The NEW Dynamics of LIFE SKILLS COACHING

 YWCA TORONTO | A TURNING POINT FOR WOMEN | United Way

Shirley Allen
Mickey Mehal
Sally Palmateer
Ron Sluser

ISBN 1-895625-02-5   (New Dynamics)

Canadian Cataloguing in Publication Data

Main entry under title:

The new dynamics of life skills coaching

Includes bibliographical references and index.

ISBN 1-895625-02-5

1.   Self-actualization (Psychology) – Study and
Teaching. 2. Life skills – Study and teaching.
I. Allen, Shirley. II. Young Women's Christian
Association of Greater Toronto

BF637.S4N4 1995 158   C95-931791-0

Other books in the Discovering Life Skills Series:

Discovering Life Skills, Volume I: Building Groups and Warm Ups	1997
Discovering Life Skills, Volume II	1980 - 2nd edition 1999
Discovering Life Skills Volume III	1983 - 2nd edition 1998
Discovering Life Skills, Volume IV: With Special Needs Groups	1986 - 2nd edition 1998
Discovering Life Skills, Volume V	1989 - 2nd edition 1994
Discovering Life Skills, Volume VI: Communicating Assertively	1991 - 2nd edition 1994
Discovering Life Skills, Volume VII: Teaching Employment Groups	1995
Discovering Life Skills Volume 8: Employability for Youth	2000

Additional copies can be purchased by calling or writing to:

The YWCA of Greater Toronto
80 Woodlawn Ave. E.
Toronto, ON M4T 1C1
Web site: www.ywcalifeskills.ca

Phone: (416) 487-7151
Life Skills Training & Publications Dept.
Fax: (416) 487-7154
Email: lifeskills@ywcatoronto.org

Published by the YWCA of Greater Toronto, 1995

Table of Contents

List of Figures

Foreword

From an idea developed in New York to the first course created in Prince Albert, Saskatchewan, in the 1960s, Life Skills training has come a long way. The YWCA of Metropolitan Toronto has been a continuing leader in the development of new Life Skills training materials from the mid-seventies and with this book now also advances the theoretical underpinnings of the training.

Life Skills training provides the learning opportunity for people to develop the skills, information and attitudes to increase their self-sufficiency in all areas of living. These self-management skills are increasingly important in these times of significant social and economic change which will test the self-reliance of many of us.

The authors are to be congratulated for this important contribution to the Life Skills literature.

D. Stuart Conger

Preface

This book is the result of a cooperative effort of many people. The authors who have been Life Skills coaches and trainers for many years, frequently discussed the need for an updated Life Skills textbook. We decided that 1995 was the time to begin writing. We shared resources and ideas, supported and confronted each other as we critiqued materials. Fortunately, we shared a common goal of producing a new text within a limited time frame and experienced much creative energy during the process. This book is the result of our work together. It represents a partnership of the YWCA of Metropolitan Toronto and Ron Sluser of George Brown College. Many people however, contributed generously and with enthusiasm to this work and they deserve recognition and thanks.

First and foremost are the NewStart authors who, in the developmental stages of Life Skills contributed articles on the theory, practise and evaluation of the methodology. These materials were published by the Saskatchewan NewStart Inc. in 1973. Many of their ideas and adaptations of their materials are included in this text. We are indebted to these men and women for the foundation they provided to the field of Life Skills. The list includes Vernon W. Mullen, D. Stuart Conger, Ralph Himsl, Mary Jean Martin, Paul Curtiss, Ronald Friedman, Terry Bersheid, Phillip W. Warren, L. Arthur Lamrock, James T. Vickaryous and Naida Waite.

A second group includes those who contributed to the writing of this book. Sande Gunning wrote the section on Efficacy and Self-esteem. Heather MacDonald designed the chart - Models

Influencing Life Skills. Shelly Altman contributed to the chapter on Evaluation. Paulette Senior assisted in developing the section on Diversity and Jan Peltier wrote the sections on Advocacy and Feminism.

A third group kindly granted us permission to reprint or adapt their written work and charts: Don Brundage and Dorothy Mackeracher for ideas from their report *Adult Learning Principles and Their Application to Program Planning*; Mary Beth Levan for her material on Spirituality and Needs in Groups; The Directors of the Association of Life Skills coaches of Ontario for their Code of Ethics, with special thanks to Tine Curran, Susan Geddis and Colleen Nadjiwon-Johnson; Harcourt Brace for Edgar Dale's model, the Cone of Experience; Prentice Hall Regents for Malcolm Knowles' chart Matching Techniques to Desired Behavioural Outcomes; Wall and Emerson, Inc. for Patricia Cranton's table Summary of Instructional Methods.

Several people have contributed to this book through their earlier writings or by acting as resource people. This list includes Carmen Simmons, Lynn Ross, Judy Miller, Paul Smith, Chris Glover, Dana Mullen, Joan Hearn and Gary Copeland. Heather McGregor and Carolyn Beatty read and commented on the manuscript helping us fine-tune our ideas. Support of another kind came from family, friends, partners and colleagues. They provided ongoing encouragement, insights and valuable feedback for our ideas.

The Life Skills team have been most helpful and patient throughout this project. Fran McCann and Annette Wijbrans merit special mention for their long hours of typing, formatting, designing graphics, their editorial guidance and for adding that special ingredient - a sense of humour. Assisting Fran and Annette were typists Juliet Fernandes and Kathleen Costello. Thanks to Betty Thompson for her ongoing support of the Life Skills department.

Finally, we offer our thanks to the thousands of participants and coaches in Life Skills groups across the country who provided the impetus for developing this approach to group work and hence the writing of this book.

Introduction

The theoretical bases for Life Skills in Canada were published, with final revisions in *The Dynamics of Life Skills Coaching* in 1973. This text has been the major source of theory for all Life Skills coaches, trainers and coaches-in-training since that time.

Although there have been a number of later studies of the Life Skills model such as Paul Smith's *Life Skills Coach Training Program,*[1] *The Taxonomy of the Life Skills Required to Become a Self-Determined Person*[2] and Dana Mullen's *A Conceptual Framework for the Life Skills Program,*[3] there has not been a comprehensive, updated publication to this time.

Life Skills in Canada today remains true to the original principles and philosophy developed in Prince Albert, Saskatchewan. Learning, through many years of practical application, with a multitude of varied Life Skills groups across this country and beyond, have helped refine and enhance the methodology.

Many of the concepts of Life Skills, such as empowerment and choice and some of the terminology such as balanced self-

---

[1]Paul Smith and Debbie White, *Life Skills Coach Training Program* (Ontario: Training Improvement Project, report #7874, Ministry of Colleges and Universities, 1979).

[2]Paul Smith, *The Development of a Taxonomy of the Life Skills to Become a Balanced Self-Determined Person* (Ottawa: Occupational and Career Analysis Development Branch, Employment and Immigration Canada, 1981).

[3]Dana Mullen, *A Conceptual Framework for the Life Skills Program* (Ottawa: Occupational and Career Analysis Development Branch, Advanced Development Division, Canada Employment and Immigration, 1981).

determined behaviour remain current today. The need for inclusive language and contemporary terminology, as well as the advent of significant social changes (feminist and anti-oppression movements as examples) require that an updated body of theory be available to Life Skills coaches and trainers.

This first edition of *The New Dynamics of Life Skills* provides Life Skills coaches, trainers and coaches-in-training with the fundamentals of Life Skills principles and the Life Skills program.

The first unit offers an historical perspective and context for Life Skills today. The principles and philosophy of Life Skills are presented in the following unit. The theoretical aspects of the methodology are covered in detail in the third section. Creativity and problem-solving skills which are essential to the model are explored in the next unit of this text. An overview of group dynamics and processes is presented in the following section. The sixth part of the book deals with the Life Skills coach and looks at the coach as a group facilitator. Also presented is a section on format, techniques, materials and one on Life Skills program planning. Evaluation, a major part of the Life Skills program is the subject of the following chapter. Finally, three bibliographies (historical, group process and group activities) complete the book.

This is a Life Skills text. Readers are encouraged to examine the many suggested group process books and resources provided in the bibliographies which contain possible stimulus and/or skills practise activities.

The cognitive understanding of the Life Skills philosophy and methodology is not sufficient to prepare an individual for coaching a Life Skills group in the community. The individual must be suitably trained by a qualified Life Skills coach trainer. This book is not meant to be a replacement for appropriate coach training, but rather as a guide for coaches, trainers and coaches-in-training.

This edition is compiled with the input from Life Skills coaches and coach trainers. It is both meant to provide updated information and evoke discussion. It is hoped that coaches and trainers will continue the dialogue regarding Life Skills with students, colleagues, agencies and funders.

This is not the final word on Life Skills, rather it is another step along the continuum. Feedback on content or lack of inclusivity from readers and the community is encouraged.

As we move to the twenty-first century, Life Skills continues to play a major role in aiding empowerment and problem-solving for individuals and groups. This text provides a cornerstone for the understanding of the Life Skills principles and Life Skills programs.

1

History of Life Skills

The roots of Life Skills ideology can be traced to observations made by Dr. Winthrop Adkins and Dr. Sidney Rosenberg while working for the Bedford-Stuyvestant (New York) YMCA. They outlined their concepts in a proposal to obtain funding from the United States Department of Health, Education and Welfare in 1964.

They conducted hundreds of in-depth interviews with "disadvantaged" adults in order to find out where they hurt, what they were afraid of and what made them feel alienated and depressed. Adkins concluded that these educationally disadvantaged adults did not respond to traditional middle class counselling methods. It appeared that they simply did not know the strategies for changing existing situations. Adkins and Rosenberg concluded that the barriers to coping with life situations effectively were both cognitive and emotional.

Adkins and Rosenberg first introduced the concept of Life Skills training in the proposal for Project Try (Training Resources for Youth), a $4.5 million anti-poverty training program. The initial program made use of problem-centred, experience based, behaviourally oriented learning groups which attempted to employ a mixture of teaching as well as counselling methods to facilitate learning. They developed a structured approach to learning through a four step lesson plan named the Life Skills Structured Inquiry Model, which included stages called The Stimulus, The Evocation, The Objective Inquiry and The Application. The lessons were presented by specially trained individuals called Life Skills Educators (LSE).

In 1965, D. Stuart Conger headed a task force to plan innovative projects for the Canadian "war on poverty". One of the proposed projects was the Canada NewStart Program. It was approved in principle by the federal and provincial ministers of Manpower, Education and Training in January 1966. This was followed by a year of negotiations between the provinces and the Federal Treasury Board and the federal-provincial relations office of the Privy Council. The federal government believed that newly created jobs would alleviate poverty, but had found that many economically poor ("disadvantaged" in their terminology) did not have the prerequisite skills to take these jobs or the problem-solving skills to maintain them. Pre-employment training programs also had not worked because the academic and occupational training was done solely from a pedagogical perspective.

In the summer of 1967, NewStart projects were established in all provinces except Ontario, Quebec and British Columbia. Each was given an initial planning grant of $100,000 for its first year plan. Each program, later funded for a five year period, had complete autonomy in achieving the goals of NewStart. The NewStart programs in Saskatchewan, Manitoba and Nova Scotia went on to research the area that later became known as Life Skills.

Manitoba NewStart did not operate for the full five years. Nova Scotia NewStart developed Dacum (Design a Curriculum) charts which could be used by Life Skills coaches. The materials produced were extensive, but very complex and difficult to implement. Further, there was not an appropriate delivery system developed. After its mandate expired, the Nova Scotia program continued for a short period of time as a private research organization.

In the summer of 1968, Stuart Conger became the director of Saskatchewan NewStart with headquarters above the Minto Bowling Alley on Eighth Street East in Prince Albert. In November of the same year, a task force under the direction of Douglas Toombs was appointed to create, develop, conduct and evaluate a Life Skills course.

Initially there was assistance from a consultant with the Thiokol Corporation which was operating a program in a US Job Corps project. This course was very much oriented to interpersonal communications. The experience was positive for the Life Skills students and they gained many communication skills, but follow up research indicated that they were still not solving problems more effectively in their personal lives.

In mid-1969, a Life Skills division was created by Saskatchewan NewStart and Ralph Himsl was appointed manager of the project which included course writers, coaches and researchers. The decision was made to follow the Adkins-Rosenberg model.

The TRY program in New York had concluded. Adkins was teaching at Columbia University and Rosenberg at York College in New York City. Adkins and Rosenberg joined the Saskatchewan NewStart team for six weeks in the summer of 1969. Although they were not lesson writers, they were excellent consultants to Ralph Himsl and the others who designed the lessons. Himsl helped develop a "second generation" of Life Skills lessons. Again, although the students who participated in these Life Skills lessons made interpersonal gains, they were still not handling problems in terms of employment or personal life as effectively as had been hoped for by program developers.

At this point, Himsl and Mary Jean Martin introduced the notion of problem-solving as an important component in the design of Life Skills lessons and the course itself. They helped shift the focus from almost a purely human relations program to one in which there was a balance of human relations, behavioural skills and knowledge. This was a problem-solving model.

They introduced a further step, called the evaluation phase of the lesson which involved students actively and constructively in the evaluation of what they learned and how they had applied what they had learned. It was felt that this would help with the implementation of problem-solving in the student's life outside the Life Skills centre. In addition, methods of behaviour rehearsal were incorporated into the Objective Enquiry phase of the lesson. (Later this was to become a separate stage, the Skills Practise phase of the lesson plan). This had the effect of making the lessons behavioural as well as cognitive. Thus evolved the "third generation" of the Life Skills course.

These developments marked a departure from the Adkins-Rosenberg philosophy and structure of Life Skills. Saskatchewan NewStart assumed that generic skills could be taught and that they would then be transferred to numerous life situations. The development of insight on the part of the trainee was seen as critical. Adkins believed that it could not be assumed that skills could or would be transferred to specific situations. He thought that students <u>must</u> learn to use specific skills in specific situations. He reasoned that eventually, as students learned a series of skills, there might be some transfer, but not a significant amount. Instead of emphasizing the development of insight, Adkins attempted to prescribe specific behavioural changes for specific situations. He advocated a rather robotic approach--one situation, one set of steps for the solution.

Adkins stressed the use of highly structured learning programs supported by multimedia kits that were designed specifically for certain groups of learners. These would be presented by a Life Skills Educator, essentially a technician who had received little training in the methodology of Life Skills.

In contrast, NewStart suggested that the course facilitator needed to be a highly trained individual with a wide range of skills and competencies. The name "coach" was chosen because coaches are associated with skill training which makes use of a wide range of instructional and motivational techniques in their training programs.

Over a period of three years, Saskatchewan NewStart devoted forty person years and $500,000 to the development of the Life Skills model. Four hundred students passed through the doors of the Life Skills Research Centre. The writers produced several works, most notably the *Life Skills Coaching Manual* containing 61 lesson plans for coaches to follow when working with Life Skills groups and *The Dynamics of Life Skills Coaching*, which outlined the philosophy, theory and techniques of Life Skills.

Final editions of the Life Skills materials were completed in 1974 and published by The Training Research and Development Station which had become the successor to Saskatchewan NewStart. It closed in 1975. Yet despite the closure, Life Skills continued to flourish and expand.

In 1971, the Federal Department of Manpower and Training (now called Human Resources Development Canada) decided to allocate $2,000,000 to sponsor field tests of the Saskatchewan NewStart Life Skills, academic upgrading and vocational training programs. Initially, this extended to seven provinces. Following this experimental phase, Canada Manpower began to use Life Skills as a basis for retraining programs across the country.

Two other organizations quickly adopted Life Skills into their programming. The first was the Canadian Penitentiary Service, which saw the potential for an effective problem-solving course for inmates in federal correctional institutions. The other was the West-Brandt Foundation of Louisiana which saw the value of the Saskatchewan NewStart program in working with high school seniors and other older adolescents.

In short order, the Northern Areas School Board in Saskatchewan, the Canadian Mental Health Association, Alberta (with the assistance of Madeline Dunkley of the Edmonton Life Skills Centre), British Columbia and Saskatchewan Welfare departments adapted Life Skills programs.

Life Skills was first introduced in Ontario at St. Clair College in Windsor. Several staff, trained by Saskatchewan NewStart in Prince Albert, initiated the Social Preparatory Program as a pilot project funded by the Ontario Government. In 1972, a provincial task force formed to look at the problem of the "disadvantaged" adult, led to a co-operative venture between St. Clair College, Canada Manpower and The Province of Ontario.
Canada Manpower purchased one hundred federally funded places (seats) at St. Clair College for a one year period.

This course known as the Basic Job Readiness Training program (B.J.R.T.) became the prototype of Life Skills programs in community colleges throughout the province and across the country. The program consisted of Life Skills training, an academic component (NewStart's Learning Individualized for Canadians [LINC]) and a vocational exploration segment. The BJRT program reflected the increased emphasis on providing training for individuals prior to their entry into retraining programs or employment.

Ann Richmond and Liz White of the YWCA of Metropolitan Toronto first introduced Life Skills to Toronto in June 1973, with the aid of a $50,000 grant from the Counselling Foundation of Canada. With additional support from a Local Initiatives Program (LIP) grant, the YWCA both collected existing resources and developed new materials which formed the basis of its Life Skills training. The first training was done with three groups of women living in Ontario Housing Corporation settings. A fourth group for "women facing a change in their lives" started in October 1974 and a widows' group and teen mothers' group began in 1975.

In September 1975, George Brown College began the initial Toronto Basic Job Readiness Training program based on a proposal written by Sandra Fishleigh, Linda Silver and Ron Sluser. By 1979, more than twenty community colleges in Ontario were operating BJRT programs and the federal government was paying $5,000,000 in training costs and student financial support.

The Life Skills concept was first brought to New Brunswick through Canadian Penitentiary system at Dorchester maximum security institution. Rick Steel, trained at Saskatchewan NewStart, was instrumental in the training of local Life Skills coaches. The Memracook Institute in St. Joseph began to train qualified coaches. By 1983, Life Skills was a prominent part of training programs sponsored by Canada Manpower. A French version of Life Skills materials was prepared and taught as well.

In 1975 Dick MacDonald and Don Anderson brought Life Skills concepts to Holland College on Prince Edward Island. Rick Steel, working with St. Francis Xavier University, along with colleagues from the Halifax YMCA, introduced Life Skills to Nova Scotia at the same time.

The Aboriginal community in Manitoba was involved with Life Skills from an early time and Rivers Manitoba was the home of the Oo za we kwun Training Centre.

Although Life Skills borrowed from several existing methodologies, the resulting concept was new and unique. Not all social service agencies and institutions were immediately convinced of the value Life Skills. As Conger states in his *Life Skills Training - A Social Invention*:

> Social inventions are notoriously slow in becoming adopted by social institutions.
> ...Someone once said that it is easier to move a graveyard than to change a curriculum...
> The same resistances to change have taken place with the Life

Skills course.[1]

There was a little uncertainty in some agencies as to exactly what Life Skills was. There was confusion between programs teaching maintenance skills or living skills and the NewStart Life Skills model. Some agency representatives presented activities such as cooking and shopping wisely as examples of skills thought to be necessary components of Life Skills training. There were some concerns that Life Skills programs would compete with group therapy. Other questions arose such as: Would funding be diverted to Life Skills? What credentials did Life Skills coaches have?

Meetings such as one held in Toronto at George Brown College in 1976 with Nancy Pridham of the YWCA of Metropolitan Toronto, Cindy Niemi of Humber College, Sandra Fishleigh and Ron Sluser of George Brown College and representatives of numerous social service agencies and institutions helped alleviate concerns and promote further understanding of how Life Skills was compatible and, in fact, complimentary to existing social service and institutional programs. They emphasized that Life Skills training in its true sense, involved behaviour change (and accompanying change in attitude), new ways of interacting, of thinking and of problem-solving.

Clarification about the differences between Life Skills and therapy groups helped break down some barriers.

> The principle difference between a therapy group and a Life Skills group can be determined by the focus of responsibility for change. If the responsibility remains with the client the process can be labelled personal growth (as in Life Skills). If the responsibility rests with the helper the approach can be called therapy. Many therapists *treat* people. Willingness to change and the responsibility for learning and behaviour lies with group members. The coach's task is to help them learn.[2]

---

[1] Stuart Conger, Life Skills Training - A Social Invention, in *Readings in Life Skills* (Prince Albert, Saskatchewan: Saskatchewan NewStart and Training Research and Development Station, 1973), pp. 3-4.

[2] Paul Smith and Debbie White, *Life Skills Training Program* (Ontario: Training Improvement Project, report #7874, Ministry of Colleges and Universities, 1979), p. 3.

In 1979, Paul Smith of Sir Sanford Fleming College in Peterborough Ontario was asked by the Ontario Government to do a study of Life Skills. His document remains as a clear description of the evolution of Life Skills. In 1981 Smith, at the request of Stuart Conger of Canada Manpower also produced *A Taxonomy of the Life Skills Required to Become A Balance Self-Determined Person*.

At the same time, Conger encouraged Joan Hearn to create updated Life Skills lessons, which she did in a publication called *More Life Skills* in 1981. She subsequently produced lessons for special needs populations and refugees. Dana Mullen, responding to Conger as well, wrote *A Conceptual Framework For The Life Skills Program* in 1985. In this publication, Mullen redefines the theoretical concepts of Life Skills methodology.

During the period from 1976 to the present (1995), the YWCA of Metropolitan Toronto has published seven volumes of Life Skills lessons in a *Discovering Life Skills* series. The lessons were developed and field-tested by YWCA Life Skills coaches in their community groups.[3] In addition, submissions were made to the manuals by coaches working with a variety of groups in diverse communities across Ontario.

At present, Life Skills programs exist in all provinces and territories in Canada. Life Skills is utilized in thousands of social service agencies and institutions, educational facilities, businesses and industry, recreational facilities and spiritual organizations. While the Life Skills structure and philosophy remain the same, there is much more flexibility in the model today. Emphasis is placed on the importance of group members identifying their own needs and setting personal goals. Personal empowerment is pre-eminent.

Outside of Canada, many countries including Britain, Australia, Sweden and the United States have implemented programs for youth and adults. Concern about youth unemployment and related problems is growing. As solutions for these youth

---

[3]In addition to the Life Skills coaches already mentioned in this text, Suzanne Killick, Marg Campbell, Jan Peltier, Lynn Ross, Mary Campbell, Mary Jane Crombie, Rachel Kampf, Lis Smith, Maureen Millard, Kit Breland, Barbara Williams, Robin Black, Maureen Eagan, Ruth Evans, June Farquharson, Mary Al Coke and Judy Bennet made contributions to the field by designing lessons for the YWCA publications.

problems are sought, new applications for Life Skills programs will continue to be identified.

Unfortunately, not all projects identified as Life Skills programs follow the philosophy and methodology. Some organizations in various parts of the country use the term, but do not adhere to the principles.

Winthrop Adkins continues to teach the *Adkins Life Skills Program* in parts of the USA using the Life Skills Structured Inquiry Learning model, with its four phases, facilitated by Life Skills Educators (LSE). Today the focus of these multi-media packages is mainly job search techniques. Adkins sometimes refers to these programs as Life Coping Skills or Life Skills Education. Life Skills in Canada places more responsibility on learning generic skills and encouraging the individual to choose goals and solutions, whereas Adkins' approach remains robotic, with each situation requiring a specific set of problem-solving skills.

The founders at Saskatchewan NewStart saw Life Skills as an important historical step leading to social advancement. Life Skills principles today remain true to their vision.

2

Philosophy and Principles

2.1 Background Assumptions

Definition of Life Skills

The term Life Skills means different things to different people. The accepted definition proposed by NewStart researchers who originated the Canadian model of Life Skills is:

> Life Skills, precisely defined, are problem-solving behaviours appropriately and responsibly used in the management of personal affairs. As problem-solving behaviours, life skills liberate in a way, since they include a relatively small class of behaviours usable in many life situations. Appropriate use requires an individual to adapt the behaviours to time and place. Responsible use requires maturity or accountability. Also, as behaviours used in the management of personal affairs, life skills apply to five areas of life responsibility identified as self, family, leisure, community and job.[1]

Assumptions about Life Skills

A course aimed at training people in Life Skills implies certain

[1] Ralph Himsl, Life Skills: A Course in Applied Problem Solving, in *Reading in Life Skills* (Prince Albert, Saskatchewan: Saskatchewan NewStart and Training Research and Development Station 1973), p. 120.

assumptions. One needs to accept that Life Skills can be:

- identified

- demonstrated

- broken down into component parts

- learned through imitation and practise

- transferred to other situations

Assumptions about Adult Learning

Life Skills methods are informed by adult learning principles developed in the 1950s and 60s. Malcolm Knowles in his book *The Modern Practice of Adult Education*[2] notes that the art and science of helping adults learn (andragogy) is based on assumptions different from those about how children learn (pedagogy). Knowles names four of these assumptions. As people mature:

- their self-concept moves from one of being dependent toward one of being a self-directed

- they accumulate a growing reservoir of experience that becomes an increasing resource for learning

- they become ready to learn something when they experience a need to learn it in order to manage real life issues in a more satisfying way

- they want to be able to apply whatever knowledge and skill they gain today to live more effectively tomorrow

Life Skills coaches need to address each of the four assumptions described by:

- encouraging and nurturing each individual to be increasingly

---

[2]Malcolm Knowles, *The Modern Practise of Adult Education: from Pedagogy to Andragogy*, Revised, (Englewood Cliffs, NJ: Prentice Hall Regents, 1980).

self-directed

- using techniques that are experiential and build on the resources that the participants bring with them to the learning situation

- creating opportunities for participants to assess their needs

- designing the program around real life applications

- organizing learning opportunities outside the group to put the knowledge and skills participants have learned into practical applications

The Concept of Skill in Life Skills

Life Skills holds that true learning, behaviourial change, occurs when learners have a clear understanding of their goals, a clear description of the new behaviour and an understanding of those conditions that make the behaviour appropriate.

A skill has the following characteristics:

- it has a definite purpose

- it can be described in terms of observable behaviour

- an increase in competency can be observed

The Life Skills Course

Many of the activities in the Life Skills course take place in a learning group composed of about ten to fifteen students with their learning guide, called a coach. The fundamental Life Skills unit is called a lesson. Coaches receive special training in the methodology and techniques appropriate for delivering a Life Skills course. Coaches have four main sources that they encourage students to make use of in their search for meaningful behaviourial change. They have:

- the resources, skills and experiences of the students

- their own experiences and training

- the resources of the community

- the materials which set out the content and goals for developing effective, self-directed, problem-solving individuals

To summarize, a Life Skills course consists of the trained coach, the students and their experiences in the community, the materials containing the content and course objectives and the resources in the community.

2.2 Philosophy and Theoretical Orientation of Adult Education

Introduction

It is important to recognize that all education is a reflection of an underlying political philosophy. It could be stated that the goal of a Life Skills program is to put into practise a democratic philosophy. Malcolm Knowles expresses it in the following way:

> A democratic philosophy is characterized by a concern for the development of persons, a deep conviction as to the worth of every individual and faith that people will make the right decisions for themselves if given the necessary information and support. It gives precedence to the growth of people over the accomplishment of things when these two values are in conflict. It emphasizes the release of human potential over the control of human behaviour. In a truly democratic organization there is a spirit of mutual trust, an openness of communications, a general attitude of helpfulness and cooperation and willingness to accept responsibility, in contrast to paternalism, regimentation, restriction of information, suspicion and enforced dependency on authority.[3]

The early writers in the field of adult education support this view with their emphasis on lifelong learning and the development of self-directed individuals. These students would be better equipped

---

[3]Malcolm Knowles, *The Modern Practice of Adult Education: from Pedagogy to Andragogy*, Revised, (Englewood Cliffs, NJ: Prentice Hall Regents, 1980), p. 67.

to move forward in a constantly changing world.

Although the approach may seem like a lofty and ambitious goal in many of Life Skills programs, it is important to keep in mind the philosophical base and guiding principles for the delivery of a Life Skills program.

Theoretical Orientations

In a report by Brundage and MacKeracher[4] *Adult Learning Principles and Their Application to Program Planning* reference is made to three sets of political orientations with their underlying assumptions about how and what adults learn. A Life Skills program may rely on any one of these approaches or a combination of all three.

Liberal

The first and most widely held orientation is based on a liberal philosophy and a pluralistic and systemic approach to teaching learning. This orientation is based on the presupposition that individuals, in response to their personal life experiences, develop a unique model of reality which represents the meanings and values they have attached to those experiences and the strategies and skills they have acquired through them. This representational model is both similar to and different from the models developed by others. Since learners bring a unique model of reality to the learning situation, they also bring unique needs and goals. The educational system, therefore, must be prepared to accept, respect and accommodate individual needs and goals.

The liberal orientation also recognizes that each individual encounters other persons and forms social groupings for mutual survival and security. Social interactions require that individuals be able to communicate their model of reality to others; be able to comprehend and acknowledge their reality; and be willing and

---

[4] Donald H. Brundage and Dorothy MacKeracher, Adult Learning Principles and Their Application to Program Planning, (Queen's Park, Toronto, Ontario: Ministry of Education, 1980), Adapted with permission pp. 7-10. These orientations are adapted from an address by Dr. Gregory Baum, Adult Education as a Political Enterprise, to the alumni of the Department of Adult Education, Ontario Institute for Studies in Education, 1978.

able to develop shared aspects of a group-defined model which is then assimilated into their own. The educational system needs to be able to facilitate this communicating, comprehending, acknowledging and sharing through group activities and social interaction. The needs and goals of the social groups are not necessarily more important than individual needs and goals; rather they are viewed as having equal importance.

The task of adult education is to provide a diverse and flexible set of programs and processes to accommodate all these individual needs rather than impose standards for content and performance.

The teaching activities are process-oriented and include helping individuals:

- create, maintain, extend and communicate their own representational model

- test and evaluate the utility of their model

- comprehend the models of others

- develop shared aspects of a group model through group activities and dialogue with others

The learning activities include:

- participating in new experiences

- discovering, extending and transforming personal models of reality

- obtaining feedback about the utility of such models

- problem-solving

- dialoguing

This orientation leads to individualized models of behaviour which function within group-defined limits. It has a tendency to value means or processes to be used in learning rather than the ends or goals to be reached. It tends to assume that individual adults are capable of adapting to the social pressures of the group without necessarily altering or reducing those pressures.

Conservative

The second orientation is based on a conservative philosophy which tends to be a more universal and traditional approach to teaching and learning. This orientation is based on the presupposition that there exists, within any given society and culture, one objective reality and ultimate truth which can be known and understood. These truths should be integrated into the knowledge, values, skills and strategies of every individual within that society or culture. The individual acquires this objective reality through assimilating standardized and public knowledge, acquiring related skills and strategies and accepting the approved values. Individuals can be evaluated by other members of their society on the basis of their ability to conform to a set of behaviourial norms which are standardized by role and status. In the ideal society, all individuals are involved in setting standards and evaluating the performance of others. In reality, these activities tend to be performed by the most powerful and influential members of the group. Sanctions are provided through law or custom to maintain the individual's commitment to this objective reality.

The task of adult education is to provide learning programs which allow all societal members to learn the basic components of the approved model of reality. The concept of universal literacy stems from this orientation (i.e., every adult *should* be able to read). Other tasks focus on the provision of autocratic structures and of learning content and criteria for judging performance.

The teaching activities are content-oriented and include:

- defining the content to be learned

- setting objectives

- planning learning activities

- presenting content

- providing feedback related to standardized criteria

- disseminating information

- modelling appropriate behaviour

The learning activities include:

- comprehending and assimilating the content

- testing out skills and strategies

- accepting and responding to feedback

This orientation leads to an objective and universal model of behaviour which is prescribed by the group. It has a tendency to value ends or goals to be reached rather than the means or processes to be used in learning. It tends to ignore the individual needs and problems of learners. It leads to consistent and competent behaviour among individuals which can be publicly certified or licensed.

Socialist

The third orientation is based on a socialist philosophy. It shares many characteristics with the liberal orientation. It also presupposes multiple individual versions of reality. As individuals develop their representational model, they tend to delete, distort, oversimplify and generalize various aspects of their experience. Some aspects become lost, repressed or misrepresented. Society itself encourages this distortion through valuing some models of reality more than others and by rejecting or discounting some. Individuals whose models of reality are undervalued, rejected or discounted tend to occupy marginal positions within society.

The task of adult education, therefore, is to provide learning programs which will assist in the recovery of lost or repressed models and traditions, to raise misrepresented aspects to a conscious level and transform them and to persuade the larger society to change its methods of dealing with these aspects.

The teaching activities are issue-, problem- or person-centred and include:

- assisting individuals through therapeutic or counselling-type processes

- assisting groups through consciousness-raising processes or through destabilizing-changing-restabilizing processes.

The learning activities include:

- self-reflecting, transforming, reintegrating

- bringing other models of reality to the attention of others

This orientation leads to the recovery of lost models and traditions and to the restructuring of misrepresented ones. It has a tendency to value separate issues and problems rather than relationships among issues and problems. In the process of recovering and restructuring certain aspects of a model of reality, it tends to discount whatever validity and utility the original model had. When used judiciously it enhances and extends the individual in positive ways and alters society in ways which enhance both individuals and society.

One example of a socialistic orientation is the *Popular Education* Method. The term "popular education" is used to describe a method and approach to learning that has been used to help people educate and organize themselves around social issues such as health care, education, nutrition. This approach was developed by Paulo Freire[5], a Brazilian educator, to teach literacy to peasants in Brazil.

The method and techniques have been adapted and used in communities across Canada and the United States. Women's groups in particular have found it to be an ideal method when working with women who experience feelings of powerlessness. The approach is humanistic, involving a methodology where the teacher becomes a student and the student becomes a teacher. People dialogue and relate to each other as equals. Participants are active rather than passive learners. Participants become empowered through this learning process. This method is based on the belief that people, if empowered, can and will make positive changes in their lives. The feminist movement is one example of how this theory of empowerment has been put into practise.

---

[5]Paulo Freire, *Pedagogy of the Oppressed*, (New York: Continuum Press, 1981).

Summary

Although these orientations are discussed here as if they were polarities which operate exclusive of each other, it is more common to find varying combinations of them within one system, one institution or even one teacher. In many cases, educators espouse one orientation for content and another for process.

Relevance to the Life Skills Orientation

The liberal orientation as outlined, fits with the democratic philosophy described at the beginning of this section. It also describes the elements of the philosophy of a Life Skills program with great accuracy.

The conservative philosophy, although very different in its assumptions, is also a helpful description of much that takes place in many Life Skills programs. On the one hand, phrases such as "one objective reality and ultimate truth" are too rigid and confining for an approach that stresses process and creative thinking; on the other hand, setting goals for the development of specific behaviourial skills suggests some assumptions about more standardized acceptable behaviours. In addition, the conservative belief stresses that people must be responsible for their own behaviour. There is also an assumption in a Life Skills program that skills can be described, modelled and improved with practise. While goals and ends are important in Life Skills, the means and process continue to be more important in a Life Skills group than in a traditional approach.

The third orientation based on a socialistic philosophy suggests that there are ways of involving participants to think critically about their daily reality and work to bring about change in society. Chris Glover in a paper *Investigating Life Skills* explores the problem of training participants in job search skills in tough economic times. Glover raises the dilemma of training people to take advantage of job opportunities that may not exist, thus adding to their record of failure. Glover notes that these issues are often not addressed in Life Skills groups. The result may be that participants put all of the blame on political and economic situations thereby negating individual responsibility to help themselves. Glover concludes,

Life skills must incorporate an investigation of the system which oppresses the participants. This would allow them a full critical understanding of their situation and how they came to be in it. At least then, understanding their past, they would be free to choose their future.[6]

Life Skills philosophy definitely embodies the principles set out in the liberal philosophy. There is room, however and in fact a need to include elements of the other two orientations, conservative and socialist. This would suggest a well rounded approach with flexibility to adapt to groups with a variety of learning needs.

2.3 Models Influencing Life Skills

Life Skills is a specific teaching/learning model with its own set of assumptions, methodologies and expected outcomes. It is a synthesis of elements drawn from a number of learning models. However, early studies indicate that Life Skills borrowed from the following:

Human Relations Training or Personal Growth Model
Medical or Therapy Model
Counselling Model
Experiential Model
Adult Education Model

A British study by G.P. Stanton et al. written in 1980, identified models from which Life Skills evolved:[7]

Deficiency
Competency
Information based
Socialization
Experiential
Reflective
Counselling

---

[6]Chris Glover, *Investigating Life Skills*, Unpublished paper, 1992.

[7]G.P. Stanton et al., *Developing Social and Life Skills* (London, England: Further Education Curriculum Review and Development Unit, 1980).

Features from all seven of the following models can be discovered in the original Life Skills program.

From the Deficiency Model: Life Skills developers identified an entire complex of inadequacies in its original target population, in interpersonal skills, problem-solving skills, knowledge of resources and self image. The course was conceived and designed with those "deficiencies" in mind.

In contrast, the current course philosophy and methodology do not focus in a negative way. In fact, the focus is on the positive aspect of skill building. The whole thrust of Life Skills is to develop abilities. As Phillip Warren writes:

> The method of training stresses behaviour and skill, not problems or motives... Emphasis on how the person can behave differently, can provide the student with a wider array of behaviours for a given type of situation or problem.[8]

From the Competency Model: Life Skills emphasizes performance of specific behavioural skills. Competence in those behaviours is not seen as an end in itself. For example, students learn attending behaviours not only for the sake of maintaining eye contact with a conversational partner, but also as one general step towards being able to communicate effectively with other persons.

From the Information Based Model: During a training course Life Skills students garner a considerable body of facts about community resources, tenants' rights and so on. The information content of the course is part of a larger objective. The task of collecting information about tenants' rights is linked with the objective of developing telephone skills, the skill of interviewing someone in authority, problem-solving skills of planning and the ability to see an argument from someone else's point of view.

There is no prescribed list of facts to be learned. Instead the particular direction an information search takes often depends on the interests and needs of the learning group.

---

[8]Phillip Warren, Behavioural Skill and Role Training Approach to Life Skills, in *Readings in Life Skills*, (Prince Albert, Saskatchewan: Saskatchewan NewStart and Training Research and Development Station,1973), p. 140.

From the Socialization Model: The Life Skills lessons contain activities that could be used as vehicles for clarifying values and promoting attitudes which would conform to societal norms. Students learn various skills for dealing with persons in authority. They also explore the expectations of employers. They examine the question of personal appearance and dress appropriate in different occupations. However, Life Skills lessons avoid any suggestion of pressure to conform. That is not their purpose. The main objectives are to practice problem-solving skills (such as brainstorming and predicting results) and interpersonal communication skills such as giving and receiving of feedback.

From the Experiential Model: In experiential learning, by combining the characteristics of learning and problem-solving into a single process, students understand how their own experience generates concepts, rules and principles to guide their behaviour. This approach initially, according to Stanton's research, seemed to have a limited place in Life Skills. However, with the growing flexibility of Life Skills and continued emphasis on the group and individuals to determine content based on their needs and experience, this model now has a valuable role in the course.

From the Reflective Model: Life Skills methodology involves learning groups where students learn and practise problem-solving and interpersonal skills. As they participate in the behavioural experience of the course, they learn to reflect on their own reactions and reactions of others, thereby gaining insight into their values, beliefs, assumptions and behaviour.

From the Counselling Model: The Life Skills program stresses the importance of the affective domain (namely, understanding and expressing feelings, values and beliefs). The design of the lesson allows for individual and group reflection on experiences in order to increase the students' self awareness of their own projected image.

2.4 A Philosophic Basis For A Life Skills Course

While Life Skills takes an eclectic approach, borrowing from other fields such as adult education, there are certain fundamental principles that describe the Life Skills philosophy. Ralph Himsl, in

Models Borrowed From	Life Skills
Deficiency	• identifies skill deficits in the target population in terms of interpersonal communication, problem-solving, knowledge of resources and self-concept formation • focuses on the positive aspect of skill-building, the development of the creation of an increasing array of behavioural choices
Competency	• emphasizes the performance of specific behavioural skills • provides a way of increasing the repertoire of skills available for use in a variety of situations
Information	• focuses on facts relevant to learners' life experiences, needs and interests taken into account in designing the content of the course • encourages learner tasks involving obtaining and collecting relevant information as an integral part of the Life Skills process
Socialization	• centres on activities for exploring values and attitudes congruent with societal norms • highlights observation, imitation and modelling as strategies for learning
Experiential	• accents an enquiry orientation that taps the experience of the learners and involves them in analyzing their experience • emphasizes action-learning techniques that use behaviour-modelling: imitation of effective behaviour; guided practice in the performance of new behaviour; recognition for learners' demonstration and application of new behaviour
Reflective	• focuses on training in reflection on each Life Skills experience, in order to develop interpersonal and intrapersonal insight • encourages the use of the written log to develop learners' recognition and recording of learning and feelings • provides opportunity to develop critical thinking skills through constructive criticism
Counselling	• attends to the affective domain • responds to need to express feeling reactions to the content of Life Skills lessons • gives opportunities for individuals to react and respond to their experiences

Figure 1 Life Skills Borrows from Other Models

an article in Readings in Life Skills[9] defines the essence of the Life Skills philosophy. His ideas are paraphrased below.

Introduction

Philosophy may be defined as a statement of general principles governing a field of activity, in this instance, the Life Skills program. Philosophical areas covered in this article are:

- objectives of the Life Skills course

- a perspective on learning in Life Skills

- the existential person and Life Skills

The Objectives of the Life Skills Course

Life Skills are defined as *problem-solving behaviours appropriately and responsibly applied in the management of one's personal affairs.* This definition states the main objectives of the Life Skills training. The course aims to train graduates who will draw from a repertoire of problem-solving behaviour to meet the problems of everyday life. To accomplish this goal, students are encouraged to learn and to practise new behaviour in and outside of the group. Problem-solving behaviour includes behaviour as specific as giving and receiving feedback, asking for help, asking questions, listening, classifying, predicting consequences, planning, brainstorming and expressing feelings. More generally, it includes skills such as recognizing problem situations, identifying assumptions, formulating alternative solutions to problems, choosing among alternatives, defining problems, carrying out plans and evaluating the effectiveness of carrying out plans and achieving goals. The extent to which the students use these new behaviours in their lives during and after completing the course is the measure of success.

The content area of Life Skills is, by definition, the management

---

[9]Ralph Himsl, A Philosophic Basis for a Life Skills Course, in *Readings in Life Skills*, (Prince Albert, Saskatchewan: Saskatchewan NewStart and Training Research and Development Station, 1973).

of personal affairs. The course defines the term "personal affairs" by describing life skills as those behaviours individuals use to manage their affairs with respect to self, family, community, job and leisure. It is important to distinguish life skills in the job area from specific job skills. For example, some job-related life skills might be exploring career preferences, job search skills and interview skills as opposed to skills such as computer, technical and accounting.

There is also a distinction between Life Skills and daily living skills. Daily living skills refer to the situation-specific basic skills an individual needs to function independently. For example, living skills are: personal hygiene, banking, cooking, cleaning and finding accommodation. While these are important and necessary skills, they are not usually included within the realm of a Life Skills course. The Life Skills method does, however, lend itself to a variety of content areas and daily living skills can be taught using the Life Skills methodology.

Adult learning theory proposes that the more concrete the experience, the greater the amount of transfer; the more abstract the learning situation, the more difficult the learning. The Life Skills course aims to provide learning situations similar to ordinary life situations. This pragmatic approach to learning encourages the transfer of skills from the classroom to life outside of the group setting.

A primary objective of the Life Skills course is to develop an effective use of problem-solving behaviour in the management of personal affairs. A secondary and yet very important objective is for individuals to become confident enough to express themselves in the discriminating use of the new behaviour they have learned. The course builds upon effective behaviour already possessed by the students by adding new behaviour to their repertoire. In the course, they identify the strengths they already have and discover strengths they may never before have recognized.

A Perspective on Learning in Life Skills

In a Life Skills course, there are two distinct meanings of learning. One meaning is the *acquisition of knowledge*. In a Life Skills group, students can acquire new information and a theoretical understanding of problem-solving. While the mental processes a student engages in may constitute learning, there is not always behavioural evidence of learning.

The second meaning of learning in Life Skills is *change in behaviour*. This happens when the students apply their new understanding to a problem-solving situation in the learning group or in their personal lives.

How does learning occur in a Life Skills group? The Life Skills theory of learning proposes a dynamic interaction of three domains for learning: *the cognitive, affective and psychomotor*. The *cognitive* is the understanding and theoretical knowledge a student acquires; the *psychomotor* is the behavioural manifestation and the *affective* is the understanding and integration of feelings in the learning process.

Role-playing is an example where there is a dynamic interplay of the three domains of learning. For example, a student learns the theory of assertive behaviour and rights (cognitive), is encouraged to consider feelings of self and others (affective) and to practise new behaviour (psychomotor). The new behaviour then leads to a new understanding and appreciation of the situation (cognitive, affective) and because assertive behaviour is usually positively reinforced, it will be repeated in similar and new situations (psychomotor).

Many of our dominant social institutions have advocated for the control, if not, suppression of feelings. The Life Skills course acknowledges the place of feelings and emotions in the learning process. It encourages the students to express their feelings about the topic under discussion and provides situations in which the students can act upon their feelings. The consideration of feelings in the learning process also admits a subjective quality to knowledge and knowledge in a pure objective sense vanishes. Since, there are not always "right" and "wrong" answers, students are encouraged to use their own unique experiences, feelings and knowledge to choose what is right or wrong for them.

Such an approach to learning legitimizes past experiences and feelings of the student. This view of learning sees the students placing their new knowledge against a unique network of emotion, experience, self-concept and cognitive style. The Life Skills coach recognizes that individuals in the group carry unique life experiences to the learning setting which affect their responses to it.

Learning involves all aspects of a person. Thus the learning, whether a mental process, an insight or new behaviour, takes on a dynamic personal quality.

The Existential Person and Life Skills

The foregoing implies an existential person who validates knowledge on the basis of subjective experience. This interpretation rejects the concept of value and truth outside the individual. The intense personal involvement of the individual in learning deliberately promotes the development of the students' use of the new knowledge, strengthening their ability to accept responsibility for their behaviours.

This philosophic disposition implies a similar orientation in course design. The definition of Life Skills as "problem-solving behaviours responsibly and appropriately used in the management of personal affairs" refers to the students being ultimately responsible for their actions. The appropriate use of problem-solving skills requires the learners to modify and adapt their behaviour to the circumstances. The lesson design emphasizes personal responsibility and accountability in the practice of the skills. The students practice skills in the "here and now". From the existential point of view, practising the skills in the here and now takes on a liberating quality. Nothing can change the past; the student can, however, learn to perform effectively in the present.

But if the students must behave responsibly toward themselves and others, how does the Life Skills course meet the requirement for training in responsible behaviour? What is the definition for responsible behaviour? Is it left to the individual to decide what is responsible or is there some acceptable internal standard for responsible behaviour?

In his historic book, *Introduction to Moral Education*, John Wilson identifies five criteria which a person's opinion must meet to qualify as a moral opinion. Wilson says that moral opinions must be <u>freely held</u>; they must be <u>rational</u>; they must be <u>impartial</u>; they must be <u>prescriptive</u> and they must be <u>overriding</u>.[10] Wilson's ideas provide a useful structure for an examination of the adequacy of the response of the Life Skills course to the need for morality or responsibility, identified in the definition of Life Skills.

In what ways do the content and the processes of the Life Skills course, providing for a "responsible" use of skills, meet these criteria for morality?

With respect to the <u>free holding</u> of an opinion, Wilson's first criterion acknowledges the place of past experiences of the students by affirming their right to decide to use the new-found skill. The message is that there is an array of new behaviours which might be helpful in everyday life, but it must be decided when, where and how to use them. The structure of the lesson provides the students with opportunities to develop their own views and to express them. The evocation phase of the lesson deliberately encourages the expression of freely-held opinions. In the application phase of the lesson, the students implement plans relating to the goals of the lesson, but make their own decisions about how, when and which plan to carry out.

The design of the objective enquiry phase of the lessons aims at creating some <u>rational</u> basis for Wilson's second criterion, opinion and attitude formation and the actions related to these opinions and attitudes. During this phase of the lesson, the students investigate and collect relevant information. They make their own judgements on the value of the information and test their developing opinions in the interactions with others in the group.

Wilson's third criterion for a moral opinion requires <u>impartiality</u>; that is, individuals must judge their actions by the same standards as they judge the actions of others. Individuals in the group see themselves as others see them and increase their observation and feedback skills to others in the group. They need the skill of questioning the effect their behaviour has upon others.

How does the Life Skills course meet these needs? The coach introduces lessons that develop self-assessment, reflective and analytic skills (by analyzing events, feelings and reactions of

---

[10]John Wilson, Norman Williams and Barry Sugarman, *Introduction to Moral Education*, (Baltimore: Penguin Books, 1967), p.77.

others in particular situations). The goal is to increase the students' perceptive powers, understanding of others and the impact of their behaviour on others. The assumption is that students will act out of an increased consideration for others when they are more self-aware.

Wilson's fourth criterion for a moral opinion requires that the opinions <u>prescribe</u> an action. The Life Skills problem-solving process relates to this criterion. The individual says: *I have considered the basis for my action, its effect upon others, its relationship to my personal need and have decided to do it!* In the course, each lesson prepares students for skill practice and application. In the part of the lesson called the objective enquiry, students examine the "facts," and consider their meaning in the context of their own needs and the effect of these actions on those around them. The problem-solving model provides a rational basis on which to act.

The responsible use of behaviour also meets Wilson's fifth criterion, the requirement for an <u>overriding</u> quality to the opinion; that is, a moral opinion takes precedence over other opinions. The individual will engage in responsible behaviour even if it contradicts the opinions of other people.

Summary

The Life Skills course provides students with training in the use of problem-solving skills in their daily lives. Students show that they have learned by demonstrating changed behaviour that is a result of a complex interplay of cognition, feeling and action. Students are encouraged to express their feelings and the Life Skills course provides them with a vocabulary to do so. Learning adds new behaviours as well as changing old ones. The Life Skills course deals with problems of the existential person in the "here and now". At the very least, the emphasis on responsible behaviour in Life Skills meets one set of criteria for moral education.

2.5 Characteristics of the Adult Learner

Facilitating a learning process is complicated; many variables must be considered to assist the learner in managing their experience.

> Perhaps the most fundamental issues to keep in mind as you read are; that learning involves a dynamic equilibrium between changes and stability; structure and process, content and activity; that learning occurs over time and within societal contexts and relationships; that adult learners have past experience, present concerns and roles relevant to work and family as well as to learning and future expectations, all of which influence learning; that adult learners bring not only their mind but also their physical body, emotional responses and cherished values to learning; and that teachers or facilitators are also adults and learners.[11]

Given that adult education in general and Life Skills courses in particular are learner-centred, it is helpful to reflect on some of the characteristics of adult learners. This information based on the work of Brundage and MacKeracher[12] is organized under the following headings:

- Self Concept
- Emotions Stress and Anxiety
- Time
- Motivation
- Learning Styles
- Stages and Transitions

Self Concept

- Adults enter learning activities with an organized set of descriptions and feelings about themselves which influence their learning processes. The descriptions are the self-concept; the feelings related to their self-esteem. Both are based on past experience and on how that experience was interpreted

---

[11]Donald Brundage and Dorothy MacKeracher, *Adult Learning Principles and Their Application to Program Planning*, (Queen's Park, Toronto, Ontario: Ministry of Education, 1980), p. 3.

[12]Ibid.

and evaluated by them.

- Adults with a positive self-concept and high self-esteem are more responsive and less threatened by learning environments and the process of change. Adults with a negative self-concept and low self-esteem are less likely to enter learning activities willingly and are often threatened by both learning environments and the process of change. Adults learn best in environments which reduce any potential threat to their self-concept and self-esteem and which provide support for change.

- When adult learners and teachers interact, their behaviour affects each other. These interactions are constructive when both are:

    - responsive to each other

    - accountable for their own behaviour

    - open to feedback from each other

    - trusting of each other

Emotions, Stress and Anxiety

- Learning involves the arousal of the human body. Minimum levels of arousal are required to create conditions necessary for conscious learning.

- Excessive arousal leads to general stress reaction, anxiety and increasing negative emotions. Distressed adults behave as if they were threatened and channel their energy in defensive behaviour. Adult learners tend to have well-organized defense systems which mask stress and its accompanying emotions. Defensive behaviour requires energy which consequently is not available for learning.

  Stress reactions which continue for too long without resolution may lead to physical and behaviourial breakdown, depression, disorientation, withdrawal, confusion, extreme agitation, dependency and poor communication.

- Past experience presents the adult learner with a paradox in the learning situation. On the one hand, stability of past experience and the learner's self-concept lead to confidence and a willingness to enter into the process of change. On the other hand, the process of change has the potential for changing the meanings, values, skills and strategies of past experience and the self-concept, thereby temporarily destabilizing both. This lack of stability may possibly lead to loss of confidence to withdrawal from the process of change.

Past Experience

- The past experience an adult learner brings to any learning activity is both a helpful resource for further learning and an unavoidable potential hindrance. Past experience is stored in memory and is assigned individualized meanings and values. These meanings, values and strategies will determine how individuals will interpret new experiences as they learn. It is helpful if adult learners are aware of their own meanings, values and strategies and how they use these to plan, make decisions, solve problems, assess information, respond to immediate experience and relate to others.

- Adult learners need to feel that their past experience is respected and valued by others. They also need to be able to respect their own past experience, to value it as a potential resource for learning and to be aware of those times when it becomes a potential hindrance to further learning.

- When adult learning focuses on the acquisition of skills and strategies, the learner must personally participate in activities in which the relevant skills and strategies are used. Learners must be aware of the limitations of their present skills and strategies and of alternative new or modified skills and strategies. Students must have a clear idea of the behaviour that constitutes the skill or strategy.

Time

- Some adults need to learn quickly and to get back to their work or family activities and responsibilities. They are often reluctant to engage in learning programs which appear to "waste their time" because the content or processes do not apply to their lives.

- When adult learning focuses on the personal problems of an individual learner, the solutions to those problems must come from their own personal values and expectations and be congruent with their personal meanings, strategies and life-style.

Motivation

- Motives are the "felt" needs with which the adult learner begins a learning activity. These may relate to unmet needs or unwanted conditions in life or to the pursuit of positive change in the direction of desired goals. Adult learners are generally more concerned with the changes they experience in the direction they have chosen and their resulting satisfaction than with meeting the standards and objectives set by others.

- Adult learners who enter a learning situation voluntarily as a result of unmet needs or unwanted conditions in their lives or non-voluntarily as a result of demands from external sources, may feel threatened and anxious about learning. Learners who enter a program voluntarily in pursuit of positive personal goals are less likely to feel threatened or anxious.

- Feedback is essential if adult learners are to modify their behaviour in an ongoing way. Feedback can only be given when learners have acted in ways which can be observed by others.

- Success in satisfying needs and reaching established objectives becomes a reinforcer for the changes already made and a motive for further learning.

Learning Styles

- Adult learners each have a preferred learning style for effecting change in their behaviour and a preferred cognitive style for processing information. Each learning style is effective in some

situations and ineffective in others. Learning styles are
independent of mental ability. There is no "one best way" for
adults to learn.

- Adult learners prefer to start with their preferred learning style
and to avoid those activities which cause them stress and
anxiety.

Stages and Transitions

- Adult learning tends to focus on the problems, concerns, tasks
and needs of the individual's current life situation. Adults are
more likely to learn in areas relevant to their current
developmental tasks, social roles, life crisis and transition
periods.

- Adult behaviour is not fixed, but changes in response to both
internal and external pressures. Adults can and do learn
throughout their entire lifetime.

2.6 Balanced Self-Determined Behaviour

Introduction

One of the primary goals of a Life Skills program is to encourage
students to develop a broader repertoire of behaviour so that they
may choose appropriate and self fulfilling responses in a variety
of situations. In a Life Skills group, participants are encouraged
to:

- develop belief systems which support their rights and the rights
of others

- practise using positive affirmations of themselves

- reduce excessive feelings of guilt, anger and anxiety

- increase the repertoire of behaviour available to them

Behaviour which enables people to act in their own best interest, to stand up for themselves without undue anxiety, to exercise their rights without denying the rights of others is called balanced self-determined behaviour (BSD). By contrast, other-determined behaviour, (OD) is characterized by ignoring one's own rights and making decisions based on others needs. Persons using selfish-determined behaviour (SD) express their thoughts and feelings but often at the expense of others.

Learning to use BSD behaviour can lead to an increase in life satisfaction and improved relationships with others. The context can vary; for example, in certain cultures, it is not acceptable to assert oneself in certain situations. However, it is generally agreed that if people go through life inhibited, bowing to the wishes of others or conversely, stepping on others in order to get their way, their feeling of personal worth will be low. Individuals who use BSD behaviour tend to be confident in interpersonal relationships, feel capable without arrogance or hostility and are basically spontaneous in the expression of feelings and emotions. They are generally looked up to and admired by others. BSD behaviour is not used to manipulate others. The goal of BSD training is to develop and maintain positive behaviour patterns and relationships.

The Importance of BSD Training

When the influences of family life, spirituality, education and business are considered, it can be seen that BSD behaviour is frequently discouraged. Sometimes BSD behaviour has been interpreted in the above institutions as SD (selfish, aggressive, pushy,) behaviour. Often those in power value OD (passive, agreeing) behaviour for others but not for themselves. Another source of confusion is the contrast between "recommended" and "rewarded" behaviour. Even though it is typically understood that one should respect the rights of others, all too often parents, teachers and supervisors contradict these values by their own actions. Tact, diplomacy, politeness, refined manners, modesty and self-denial are generally praised. Yet to "get ahead" it is often acceptable to "step on" others.

In the family, children are frequently censored if they speak up for their rights. Admonitions such as: *Don't you dare talk to your mother (father) that way, Children are to be seen, not heard, Never let me hear you say that word again*, are not conducive to a child's assertion of self.

Teachers and schools also discourage BSD behaviour. Quiet, well-behaved children who do not question the system are rewarded, whereas those who challenge the system are often dealt with sternly. Many educators believe that a child's natural and spontaneous desire to learn is lost by the fourth or fifth grade. Some educators believe that this loss of spontaneity is a result of restrictions on self-expression.

In the workplace, further inhibitions to healthy self-expression occur. Employees become aware in many organizations that one must not do or say anything that will "rock the boat". In hierarchical organizations, the boss is "above", others are "below" and there are norms of behaviour and expectations to conform. Employees quickly learn to be "company people", to keep things running smoothly and to have few ideas of their own. In some organizations, it is often not acceptable or safe to behave in a BSD manner. There is now, however, a trend in some workplaces toward a more democratic philosophy. Ideas such as participatory management, profit sharing, empowerment and self-directed work teams are now being advocated by some companies. Interpersonal skills are now recognized as key skills, which are as and perhaps more, important than technical skills for success on the job. The individuals who can display BSD behaviour are and will be increasingly valued for their contributions to the workplace.

In some contemporary spiritual communities, the focus on the self and meeting one's own needs is contrary to religious teachings. Qualities such as humility, self-denial and self-sacrifice are fostered to the exclusion of standing up for oneself. However, being assertive(BSD) does not have to be incongruent with the teaching of spiritual groups. Healthy self-expression and attention to one's own needs can produce a balanced, fulfilled individual.

It is common for persons who have been selfish or aggressive in a given situation to feel some guilt as a result of their behaviour. It is less widely recognized that a person using BSD behaviours can also experience guilt produced by childhood conditioning. The institutions of society have so carefully taught inhibiting expression of even one's reasonable rights, that people may feel guilty or selfish for having stood up for themselves.

Families, schools, businesses and religious institutions have tended to undermine BSD behaviour. The contention of BSD training is that people have the right to express themselves as long as they do not hurt others in the process.

Definitions

Figure 2 compares BSD, OD and SD behaviour.

As outlined in the figure, the other-determined (OD) response in a given situation is typically non-assertive and self-denying. The individuals are inhibited from expressing true feelings, seldom achieving their desired goals and allowing others to choose for them. They often feel hurt and anxious as a result of their inadequate behaviour. Decisions are based on the needs of others.

Persons who are selfish-determined (SD) may reach their goals at the expense of others. Their decisions are based solely on their own needs. Although SD behaviour can feel self-enhancing and expressive at the time, it usually results in hurting others by making choices for them, minimizing their worth as persons. SD behaviour commonly results in a lack of concern or a "put down" of the other. The other person's rights have been denied and they may feel hurt, defensive and humiliated.

In contrast, ideal balanced self-determined (BSD) behaviour is appropriately assertive and self-enhancing and involves an honest expression of feelings. BSD behaviour takes into account the individual's needs and the needs of other. BSD behaviour leads to individuals often achieving their goals, having chosen for themselves how they will act. In certain circumstances, BSD behaviour may include making conscious decisions based on the needs of others or solely on the individual's own needs. The key consideration is that BSD behaviour is a choice. Typically, people feel good when they have behaved in a balanced self-determined manner.

When the outcome of these three contrasting behavioural approaches are viewed from the perspective of the other person (i.e., the individual toward whom the behaviours are directed), a pattern emerges. Other-determined behaviour often produces feelings ranging from pity to outright contempt by the other person. Selfish-determined behaviour leads to pain and

	OTHER-DETERMINED BEHAVIOUR (OD)	SELFISH-DETERMINED BEHAVIOUR (SD)	BALANCED SELF-DETERMINED BEHAVIOUR (BSD)
BEHAVIOUR	• self denying • avoids conflict • allows other to choose • intimidated by others • reactive • makes decisions based on other's needs	• expressive (at the expense of others) • creates conflicts • chooses for others • insensitive to other's feelings and wishes • creates tension • decides solely on own needs • unaware of others needs	• honest and direct • willing to compromise • makes choices for self • considers other's rights and feelings • respectful of others and self • can be SD or OD at times by choice
FEELINGS	• frustrated • anxious • hurt • resentful • inferior	• righteous • hostile • superior • unfeeling	• feels good about self • confident • self satisfied
RESULTS	• does not achieve desired goal • relationships deteriorate	• achieves goal by hurting others • alienates others	• may achieve desired goal • satisfying and caring relationships
OTHER PERSON'S FEELINGS	• pity • irritation • guilt • anger	• hurt • humiliated • defensive • angry	• respect • feels valued

Figure 2 A Comparison of Balanced Self-Determined Behaviour, Other-Determined Behaviour and Selfish-Determined Behaviour

humiliation for the other person, whose response will range from fear to anger and retaliation. In contrast, a transaction involving BSD behaviour allows for self-expression and achievement of goals of both the self and the other person.

BSD behaviour is situational in nature. That is, most people feel able to handle some situations assertively and have difficulty only with certain situations. or, they may have difficulty with certain categories of people such as authority figures. Also, the ability to use BSD behaviour varies with the context and time in a person's life.

The basic premises of BSD training are that:

- change is possible

- since behaviour is learned, it can be unlearned

- behaviour can be broken down into skills which can be learned and practised

- BSD training can be useful to anyone; individuals can be at different places on the continuum of OD to BSD to SD depending on the situation

- BSD training increases the repertoire of choices, enhancing sense of self and relationships with others

BSD behaviour is for all who wish to improve their quality of life and their interpersonal relationships. It is important for Life Skills coaches to be role models of BSD behaviour, recognize its validity and apply its principles in facilitating the personal growth of participants in Life Skills groups.

The Pendulum Swing: The Process of Learning New Skills

Beverly Gaw, in an article entitled *The Pendulum Swing: A Necessary Evil in the Growth Cycle*[13], explains how attempts to change one's behaviour to become a more BSD may be thwarted by comments such as: "What's wrong with you? You used to be so easy going! You never used to rock the boat". Participants need support when they try out new behaviour and the Life Skills coach will find it helpful to have a framework for understanding the process of assimilating a new behaviour.

Gaw defines the pendulum swing as a simple matter of overcompensation or over learning. When practising new behaviour and improving their self-concept, learners can sometimes exhibit selfish or aggressive behaviour (SD). Their behaviour does not swing immediately from other-determined (OD) to self-determined (BSD), but rather to selfish-determined behaviour.

Another likelihood for people practising BSD behaviour is that they do it indiscriminately without taking into account the question of appropriateness and accountability. However, with ongoing practise, support and reflection, the new behaviour becomes integrated as a choice in a person's repertoire. The options for choosing from a variety of responses to a specific situation are increased and the locus of control for making the decision is with the individual. Participants will eventually experience less anxiety and fear. They may describe themselves as feeling more centred, grounded or empowered.

The pendulum swing then, is an important concept to understand the sometimes erratic process of growth and change. Participants need to understand that when changing their behaviour, they may feel awkward or unnatural. It is important to reassure them that these feelings will pass with time and experience.

---

[13]Beverly Gaw, The Pendulum Swing: A Necessary Evil in the Growth Cycle, in *The Annual Handbook for Group Facilitators*, ed. John E. Jones and J. William Pfeiffer, (California: University Associates, 1979).

2.7 Efficacy and Self-Esteem

Albert Bandura's Contributions to Life Skills Methodology

A discussion of Life Skills Methodology in the 1990s would be incomplete without acknowledging the influence of Social Learning Theorist Albert Bandura. Many of the concepts that experienced and neophyte coaches accept as central to the Life Skills learning process (such as: modelling, vicarious learning and self-efficacy) can be directly traced to Bandura's research.

Throughout his career in the field of psychology and specifically Social Learning Theory, he has studied and published prolificly about concepts such as behaviour modification, modelling, observational learning, self-regulatory processes and self-efficacy.

Bandura's early and later work provide a "bridge" in the field of psychology. He finds that both traditional psychodynamic and traditional learning theories are insufficient to explain behaviour and personality. He believes that behaviour can best be understood by considering that it is influenced by both personal and environmental variables.

Bandura believes that a fuller understanding of behaviour could be provided by acknowledging the notion of Reciprocal Determinism. That is, that all three variables - the person, the behaviour and the situation - influence each other. The traditional definition of Life Skills states that appropriate use of Life Skills requires an individual to adapt behaviour to time and place. It is in this definition that the relevance of Bandura's work can be seen. Life Skills coaches emphasize to participants that in learning new behaviour/skills, it is essential to consider the setting in which people may be practising new behaviour. It is acknowledged that individuals are impacted by their environments in different ways that affect their ability to change behaviour, learn new information and skills as well as practise them. Also, it is in the practise of these skills that the individuals will change their environment, which then impacts again on individuals and their behaviour.

Learning Theory

Traditional conditioning theorists like Skinner and Hull place a great deal of emphasis on the importance of "reinforcement" for learning or behaviour change to occur. Bandura accepts that reinforcement is important; however, he does not regard it as the only way that behaviour is acquired, practised and/or learned. He believes that people can learn merely by observing others and then trying it out for themselves. Learning by modelling is commonplace in Life Skills groups. Many participants report that it was their observation of another student's competence in a particular skill that prompted them to practise the skill themselves.

Bandura also expands on the notion of reinforcement. He believes that people's behaviour could be influenced by both actual reinforcement and Anticipated Reinforcement. In a Life Skills group, students may be "rewarded" by other group members for their "risk-taking" behaviour which then may reinforce them to take more risks in the group. As well, students may anticipate that aggressive behaviour such as bullying and yelling at their peers may elicit an unfavourable response. They do not have actually to engage in the aggressive behaviour and experience other's negative reinforcement in order to learn to avoid this behaviour. People can anticipate or predict responses to behaviour. Again in the Life Skills setting, this provides the student with the opportunity to set goals based on an exploration of appropriate time and place.

Bandura's theories support Life Skills coaches in acknowledging that people are feeling, thinking beings who use images, thoughts and plans. Most people can and do set goals, regulate behaviour through internal standards and are able to foresee, anticipate and predict the consequences of that behaviour. The phases of the Life Skills lesson plan provide opportunities for students/participants to learn and change behaviour based on the processes described above. Referring back once again to the traditional definition of Life Skills - Bandura's beliefs embrace the concepts of responsible use, maturity and accountability.

One of the key concepts of Bandura's Social Learning Theory is the process of Observational Learning. Previous researchers and theorists had written on the subject of imitation but Bandura expands on this for the purposes of understanding learning.

Observational Learning is just that: learning new behaviour through observing the behaviour of others. It is more than imitation however, because it is known that people will be discriminating and will learn from different models.

Bandura[14] (1977) describes observational learning as a four stage process. The first stage consists of Attentional Processes. People learn through observation only if they have the opportunity to "attend" to the model's behaviour. This also consists of learners being able to recognize important aspects of the behaviour and to differentiate among its distinctive features. The second stage involves Retention Processes. In order to learn and practise a new behaviour people must be able to "recall" the model's behaviour and be able to remember the critical elements of it. Often people will use mental images or verbally code the model's actions. For example, the students' first attempt at the skill of confrontation may be based on their observation of confrontation demonstrated by another member. They may try to conjure up an image of the previous successful interaction as well as "talking" themselves through it ("Remember to ask if they want feedback...my non-verbal behaviour should be congruent with my words...ask if they need any clarification...etc). The third stage Motor Reproduction Processes is where the individuals put the mental images and verbal cues into practise. Time, effort and practise are usually critical to this stage. The fourth stage Motivation Processes is very important to the observational learning process. That is, with motivation all of the other stages are powerful determinants of the acquisition and performance of complex social behaviour. But without motivation the learning process suffers. The Life Skills process acknowledges that motivation is a subjective state which cannot be assessed by anyone but the learner.

In Life Skills groups both active and observational learning is encouraged. The group has as many "models" of behaviour/skills as there are numbers of participants. Bandura's concepts of Vicarious Learning and Vicarious Reinforcement are also integral parts of the Life Skills process. When students observe other students being reinforced for their behaviour, this also serves as reinforcement to the observer. The group format of Life Skills supports and encourages much vicarious learning. Anecdotally, it

---

[14]Albert Bandura, *Social Learning Theory* (New Jersey: Prentice Hall, 1977).

has been referred to as the "osmosis" method by some coaches. It is generally accepted that an individual's behaviour in the group will not be the only predictor of behaviour outside of the group.

Some views of reinforcement suggest that almost all human behaviour is influenced by "external" rewards and punishments. This is not necessarily Bandura's view. His perspective is one that takes into account the possibility of "self-reinforcement". He believes that in addition to being governed by external rewards and punishments, an individual's action is also governed by Internal Standards. Bandura believes that personal thoughts, feelings and actions are heavily influenced by both the positive and negative reinforcements individuals give themselves. This concept is constantly taught and nurtured in the Life Skills process. That is, the individual students set their own goals, based on their feelings, experiences and expectations. While feedback (the feelings and opinions of others) is important, self assessment is just as highly valued. The Life Skills process provides members with the opportunity to explore their internal standards and assess their behaviour in relation to them.

In Bandura's later work[15], he increasingly emphasizes the role of Self-Efficacy. Self-efficacy is simply the belief that people have about their ability to "master" a particular behaviour successfully. For example, it would be very difficult for students to practise "assertive communication" if they did not believe that they were "capable" of being assertive.

Bandura believes that people act or decide on courses of action based upon their estimate of their own self-efficacy. It is important for the Life Skills coach to understand the power of self-efficacy in behaviour change. Much emphasis is placed on helping students to assess their efficacy levels and to raise these levels. For example, coaches can ask students to rate their efficacy levels for a particular skill using a scale of one to ten. Students can be encouraged to explore their confidence or efficacy levels through internal measures, both physical and emotional. The following can be considered as a partial list of measures to be considered:

- awareness of the level of anxiety or comfort people feel when

---

[15]Albert Bandura, The Self System in Reciprocal Determinism, *American Psychologist*, Vol. 37, 1992, pp. 122-147.

contemplating a particular task

- awareness of the level of anxiety or comfort people feel when practising or using a particular skill

- awareness of physical reactions, such as sweaty palms, heart racing, flushing

Feedback by the coach and other participants is also an extremely critical element for students who are attempting to assess or raise their efficacy level in a particular skill. It provides students with the opportunity to check out their own perceptions of their emotional and physical awareness with that of the others. In the practising of new skills, students who receive feedback often learn that they may be more proficient than they believed themselves to be. They may also learn that there are easier ways to go about a particular task. When a task does not appear as formidable, a student's efficacy level is increased.

If students have assessed their own abilities incorrectly they may fail or not be able to achieve the desired behaviour. However right or wrong, people do act on the basis of an assessment of their own capabilities. People's judgements will also determine how long they will persist and how much negative reinforcement they will endure in attempting to carry out the task.

Bandura believes that self-efficacy will also determine how extensively people will prepare themselves for tasks and behaviours they will actually select. Many other researchers have built on Bandura's theories regarding self-efficacy in helping people to change substance abusing behaviour. An understanding of self-efficacy is central to Life Skills coaching and the learning process that students participate in. It is as important as other optimal learning conditions such as improving self-esteem and motivation to change.

2.8 Feminism

The development of Life Skills methodology coincided with the most recent waves of feminism. The two share many philosophical tenets - personal empowerment, dignity, freedom of choice, equal access to opportunities, acceptance of differences, search for control over destiny and the relationship between rights and responsibilities.

bell hooks defines feminism as:

> a commitment to eradicating the ideology of domination that permeates Western culture on various levels - sex, race and class, to name a few - and a commitment to reorganizing society, so that the self-development of people can take precedence over imperialism, economic expansion and material desires.[16]

Deborah Aslan Jamieson states that feminism:

> is the desire and struggle for freedom, [which is the same for each of us - Black, Latina, Native American, etc.] - even though our methods may differ.[17]

Given the basic inequities in North American society, it is critical that the Life Skills model embrace a woman-positive approach and that coaches understand and promote the connection between the two philosophies.

2.9 Diversity

We are living, learning and working in an increasingly diverse society where differences exist on countless levels: race, national or ethnic origin, colour, gender, age, sexual orientation, religion, physical and/or mental ability, life experience, status (economical, marital, family),... and much more than can be listed. Aspects of these differences are often encountered on a daily basis.

Today, through social, economic and even political trends, there is increased interaction among members of traditional mainstream society and marginalized groups. With this increase in interaction among diverse groups comes the need to learn about and appreciate the values and contributions of all group members to

---

[16]bell hooks, in *A Feminist Dictionary*, (London: Pandora, 1990), p. 159.

[17]Deborah Aslan Jamieson, in *A Feminist Dictionary*, (London: Pandora, 1990), p. 159.

maximize learning. This process can help prepare participants for a changing world.

These changes provide both the challenge and opportunity for Life Skills coaches to integrate objectives of:

- responding to socio-economic changes

- modifying and adapting Life Skills lessons to be sensitive to the norms and values of diverse groups

- modifying training materials

This challenge taken seriously, suggests the need to look at the very fabric of our institutions to include assessing various aspects such as human resources policies as well as program design and delivery. It is beyond the scope of this book to discuss in detail all the implications of putting the above statement into action. However, the intention herein is to heighten awareness and celebrate the richness that diversity brings to Life Skills groups.

In general terms however, the following can be included in a Life Skills program:

- understanding of how differences can impact on behaviour

- heightening awareness and sensitivity to diversity

- confronting biases and stereotypes

- exploring strategies for making communities places where diversity can be valued and fostered

The assessment of materials is dealt with in Unit 6 in more specific terms.

2.10   Spirituality

Many people come to the group with spiritual needs. This does not mean that people are basically "religious". Rather "spiritual" refers to humankind's need to see and feel a part of the creative process of living. Questions often asked might be: *What is the purpose of life? What is the right way to live? Are people good or bad? Is there a god in charge of this world? Are there other worlds besides the one we know?* There are no factual answers to these kinds of questions. Each culture answers them in its own way.

Values Clarification is the method used in Life Skills for the examination of personal beliefs. There are many exercises and activities designed to help people discover their fundamental biases, assumptions, attitudes and values.

Group members need to see their own concerns and confusions as legitimate. They need to see that people hold a variety of beliefs as they travel through life. But individuals must have the freedom to pursue answers on their own initiative without being judged by others.

Individuals from varying perspectives help students appreciate the diversity of opinion that exists. In the final analysis, each individual reaches a personal position.[18]

---

[18]Mary Beth Levan, *Lodestar: Life Skills Coach Training Manual* (Northwest Territories: Native Women's Association, 1986). Adapted with permission.

2.11 Ethics

Life Skills coaches must have a clear understanding of the ethical issues involved in group work. The following reprint is one example of a code of ethical conduct.

Association of Life Skills Coaches of Ontario Code of Conduct[19]

Introduction

The profession of Life Skills coaching is dedicated to providing an environment in which individuals can freely choose to acquire the skills necessary to function appropriately and successfully in their own lives. It is not possible to foresee every situation the Life Skills coach may encounter. Life Skills coaches must exercise personal judgement and ethical reflection.

Section I Responsibility to Group and Individuals in It

Coaches will regard the well-being of the groups they facilitate as their primary responsibility.

Coaches shall only undertake group or individual facilitation that they honestly believe they are capable of handling.

Coaches shall recognize that competence for a particular task may require advice or collaboration with experts in other professional fields, on a confidential basis. It is professionally ethical to obtain this advice in such instances, following the proper legislative procedures.

Coaches will respect group members in professional relationships with them and act in accordance with the members individual needs and appropriateness in the coaching situation.

---

[19]Reprinted with permission of the Directors of the Association of Life Skills Coaches of Ontario.

Life Skills coaches must be aware of the diverse backgrounds of group members and, when dealing with topics that may give offense, treat the material objectively and present it in a manner for which the individual is prepared.

The Life Skills coach should be open, honest and non-judgemental. Coaches must be mindful of their biases and values as they reflect on members of the group and maintain confidentiality at all times.

Coaches shall take into account the individual's motivation, capacity and opportunity for change at any given time during the change process to appropriately guide the interaction.

A coach's commitment to professional values does not exclude the coach from participating in outside interests such as politics, another profession, occupation or business enterprise. Coaches shall not allow outside interests to occupy their time such that participants suffer from inattention or poor service. The coach shall disclose the nature of the conflict to the participant(s) when necessary.

Coaches shall recognize that behaviour is not the individual and that the individual has the right to change his behaviour if he/she chooses. Care must be given so that the individual's choice for self determination is maintained.

Coaches shall remember that the participant is not expected to demonstrate behaviours beyond their capacity and their level of skill development. The coach shall strive to present various learning opportunities for the development of the required skills to enable the individual to make the required behaviour change.

In the case of voluntary or involuntary termination of the participant/coach relationship, the Life Skills coach's goal should be that the student be allowed to leave with as much dignity as possible.

Section II Responsibility to the Employer

Coaches will fulfill obligations to group members and responsibilities to their employer with integrity and competence. Integrity is a fundamental part of a Life Skills coach's practice.

Coaches shall inform their employer of any situation that may impede their competent performance or infringe on their integrity.

Coaches are accountable and responsible for the efficient performance of their duties to their employers as well as providing participant and group process.

Section III Responsibility to the Community

Advertisements and other public notices relating to Life Skills made by Life Skills coaches shall be clear and true and not misleading. Reference to the Association of Life Skills coaches Accreditation process or other association/organizations shall not be used in any advertising unless written permission is received.

Section IV Responsibility to Self

In private life or professional activity, a coach's behaviour reflects upon the profession as a whole. This behaviour shall not impair the coach/participant relationship.

Life Skills coaches carry a heavy social responsibility as their recommendations and professional actions may alter the lives of others. The coach shall be careful in situations that may lead to misuse of their influence.

Coaches must be mindful of their biases and values as they reflect on members of the group.

Part of a professional Life Skills coach's competence is to maintain his/her own physical and psychological well-being.

Coaches shall be careful in expressing their view on the findings, opinions and professional conduct of colleagues, confining such comments to matters of fact and matters of their own knowledge.

Coaches should strive continuously to upgrade their knowledge, skills and abilities in their professional service through life long learning.

The profession's focus should be the groups and the individuals in the group. This focus assumes that a Life Skills coach maintains a high degree of self-awareness so that he/she can recognize when personal needs, feelings, values and limitations interfere with the process of planned change and/or termination of a professional relationship.

Coaches shall assist their proper function and effectiveness by participating in on-going professional development, continuing in and contributing to Life Skills coaching knowledge and education, liaison with colleagues and other professional associations relevant to their field.

Section V General Responsibility

Coaches shall recognize the intense level of affective involvement inherent in a professional relationship, therefore, coaches must ensure that the difference between professional and personal involvement with students is explicitly understood and respected and the coach's behaviour is appropriately professional.

Coaches defending themselves against allegations of malpractice or misconduct are responsible for contacting the Association of Life Skills coaches of Ontario as soon as practicable in order to obtain the necessary support in their defense.

Section VI Responsibility of Confidentiality

Coaches shall protect the privacy of participants according to the current laws and hold in confidence all professionally acquired information concerning the participants. Coaches will disclose such information only when authorized by the participant or when obligated legally to do so.

Coaches shall allow individuals to be the primary source of information about themselves and their issues.

Coaches shall realize that personal information can be used in a court of law and that rules governing the record of information be adhered to.

As a general principle, participants have the right to know what their records contain and should be permitted the opportunity to check the accuracy of all factual data.

Confidential information may only be divulged with the prior written consent of the individual concerned, specific to the agency or individual enquiring.

When disclosures is required by law, by order of a court or competent jurisdiction or by the work setting. Coaches shall not divulge more information than is required and when possible notify the participant of this requirement.

Coaches shall endeavour to promote and maintain excellence in the profession of Life skills coaching by adhering to these confidentiality standards.

3

The Theory of Life Skills

3.1 Definition

Life Skills are problem-solving behaviours appropriately and responsibly used in the management of personal affairs. Effective Life Skills might be defined as internalized sets of attitudes and behaviours which can be applied in all areas of life: self, family, leisure, community and job. The life skills model is a multi-dimensional learning system that facilitates the life-long acquisition of generic skills (personal management, problem-solving, communications and critical thinking) which enable people to function effectively in their personal and professional lives.

3.2 Relevance

The NewStart Life Skills model was initially designed to meet the learning needs of "socio-economically disadvantaged" adults who were viewed by developers as a separate, identifiable group in society. Ralph Himsl, a NewStart programmer, described the intended population in 1973:

> Study of the literature and direct observation reveal that many disadvantaged have a complex interlocking set of inadequate behaviours. Some lack the skills needed to identify problems, to recognize and organize relevant information, to describe reasonable courses of action and to foresee consequences. They often

fail to act on a rationally identified course of action, submitting rather to actions based on emotion or authority. Often they do not benefit from experience since they do not evaluate the results of their actions...They lack the self-confidence to develop their abilities...They lack effective ways of seeking help from each other and agencies. They have ineffective interpersonal relationships and lack basic communications skills.[1]

The intended group for Life Skills training has radically changed with the evolution of Life Skills. As Paul Smith states:

Problem-solving is a critical function in daily living and all too frequently individuals do not have an adequate skill level in problem resolution. As Life Skills continues to develop, it is used more and more in a variety of contexts, in fact, in any situation in which individuals have problems they desire to solve.
Thus, it may be more meaningful to state that many individuals can benefit from Life Skills training if there is a need and a willingness on the part of those individuals to either develop new problem-solving skills or to improve on existing skills, so that they will be able to deal more effectively with life situations.[2]

Today it is recognized that Life Skills training is adaptable to a broad spectrum of interests without compromising the system's integrity. It can benefit both advantaged and marginalized populations.

Life Skills training is most effective with willing participants who want to enhance their problem-solving skills as opposed to those who are mandated or are coming for remuneration. Similarly, because of the need for transferability, (from the group to personal life) Life Skills is more effective with those who can conceptualize, work with abstract ideas and are capable of having insight. Finally, Life Skills benefits those participants who are rooted in reality, that is who are not actively psychotic, heavily medicated or under the influence of mood-altering chemicals.

---

[1]Ralph Himsl, *Readings in Life Skills* (Prince Albert, Saskatchewan: Saskatchewan NewStart and Training Research and Development Station, 1973), p. 15.

[2]Paul Smith, *Life Skills Coach Training Program* (Ontario: Minister of Colleges and Universities, T.I.P. No. 7874, 1979), p. 15.

3.3 Objectives

The purpose of Life Skills training is to assist individuals to think through problems for themselves and to make their own decisions. The ultimate outcome is not necessarily a better solution for the particular problem, but rather greater confidence and more skill development on the part of the individual group member.

The intent of the training is to increase a person's freedom of choice. The emphasis is on personal learning, which includes an ability to manage one's life effectively and with more confidence.

The main objective of the Life Skills program is to develop graduates who will draw from a repertoire of problem-solving behaviours to meet the problems of everyday life. A further objective is for individuals to develop balanced self-determined behaviour along with an ability to be discriminating in using BSD behaviour in the community.

Balanced self-determined behaviour means persons choose their behaviour freely and exercise self-control. They have integrated the concept of personal value, signifying that both they themselves and other persons are equally worthy of justice and respect.

Life Skills training in its true sense, involves behaviour change (and accompanying change in attitude), new ways of interacting, of thinking and of problem-solving.

3.4 The Life Skills Model

The Life Skills educational model as illustrated in Figure 3 is an integrated system that has a number of components. First, it is a theoretical model, which has a basis in modern psychology and adult learning theory. Second, it is a content model through which coping, communication, critical thinking and problem-solving skills are developed. Third, it is a methodological model which provides the framework and techniques for effective skills development. Fourth, Life Skills is the interaction of all of these elements, enhanced by the interplay of group dynamics that are brought to the model via the participants.

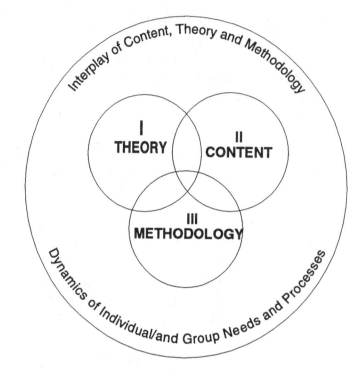

Figure 3 The Life Skills Educational Model

Theoretical Orientation

The Life Skills approach begins with the premise that learning is change; change that begins and ends with the learner and change that is relevant to the learner. Hence, learners set their own goals and evaluate their personal performance. Through a process of examining alternatives and ways to achieve goals, they decide upon an avenue of appropriate and responsible change that is both realistic and achievable.

Another premise is that because our actions impact others, the objective of Life Skills training is to achieve a level of personal performance that strikes a balance between our own recognized needs and the needs of others, in order to accommodate all parties. In other words, balanced self-determinism.

The original NewStart developers identified three integrated domains within the learner: affective (feeling), cognitive (intellectual) and psychomotor (physical, behavioural). Effective change or development occurs when all three elements are addressed in the learning process. This holistic approach is fundamental to the Life Skills model.

The developers also recognized that individuals exist in relationship with other human beings and that interaction is fundamental both to making and reinforcing change. Therefore, the Life Skills model utilizes a small group process as its vehicle.

The Life Skills learning model requires alternation of abstract thinking and application or doing. Abstraction yields understanding; application yields changed behaviour. Self-exploration leads to self-understanding and action, which in turn solicits feedback on the action, to further self-exploration and so on. The more understanding, the more action, the more changed behaviour (see Figure 4).[3]

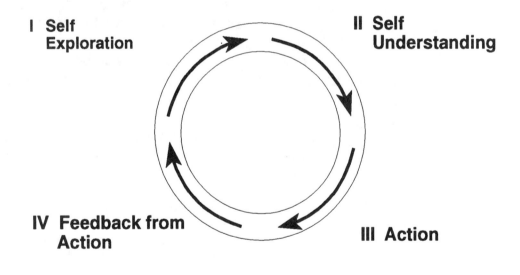

I Self Exploration

II Self Understanding

IV Feedback from Action

III Action

Figure 4 The Cyclical Process of Increasingly Effective Functioning

In this spiralling cycle, self-exploration leads to self-understanding, which is manifested in action. Feedback from the

---

[3]Paul Curtis and Phillip Warren, *The Dynamics of Life Skills Coaching* (Prince Albert, Saskatchewan: Saskatchewan NewStart, 1973), p. 113.

action leads to further exploration, increased understanding and new more effective actions.

Integrated learning and behavioural change occur when learners have a clear understanding of their individual goals, a clear description of new behaviour and the conditions which make the behaviour acceptable.

Finally, the multidimensional aspects of the Life Skills model require specialized training for practitioners in order to maintain the integrity of the system. Therefore, coaches are trained to work with the Life Skills model, to facilitate group process and to model the skills of behavioural counselling. The role of the Life Skills coach is discussed in depth in Unit 6.

Content

In the Life Skills model, process rather than the content of the training distinguishes it from many other training models. The content provides guidelines around which the coach organizes learning activities. Content falls into five areas: self, family, community, employment and leisure, each being an area that contributes to a balanced life. These five areas are inclusive of all parts of a person's life.

Sue Geddis, in a 1994 paper suggests that there are really four areas of life responsibility: family, community, employment and leisure. She states:

> The self is the pivotal mechanism around which everything else turns. That is what we are aiming for and that is the balanced self-determined person. The self can choose behaviour which bring the balance between the outside world and the world within the self.[4]

To function effectively in each of these areas of life requires certain generic skills, which are transferable from one circumstance to another. These skills are identified and defined in detail to form the basis of the Life Skills lesson objectives.

---

[4]Sue Geddis, Paper Delivered at ALSCO Conference (Orillia, Ontario: 1994).

The degree of competency a learner has in a specific skill is examined in behavioural terms within a structured lesson plan so that a new skill can be developed through a process of behavioural change. Acquisition of these individual skills forms the necessary foundation for the development of more complex competencies: for example, personal management skills, problem-solving skills, communications skills and critical thinking skills ...which are essential to life-long learning.

Wherever possible, the source of the lesson content focuses on problems relevant to the learner. In any Life Skills group, there are a number of predictable problem situations which arise, such as dealing with conflict. The Life Skills course consists of pre-planned learning experiences that focus on these typical problems. However, members of the learning group are often dealing with life situations unique to themselves. If these problems are relevant to the group at that time and if they lend themselves to the Life Skills process, the coach might use them as a focus for the lesson.

Thus the content consists of both pre-planned experiences and problems that students or the Life Skills coach bring to group. The aim is the development of learning processes. The course content is not the end of learning, but a means to it.

The Concept of "Breaking Down" Skills

In the Life Skills model and in Life Skills training, emphasis is placed of the commonality of generic skills rather than the uniqueness of situations or problems. Unlike the model offered by Adkins and Rosenberg in the United States, in which each problem has a specific set of steps for a solution, the NewStart model focuses on students learning generic skills which can be transferred to many situations.

Having to perform during a job interview is not a skill per se, but rather an application of many generic skills that deal with a complex problem situation. Some examples of skills required for the job interview might be active listening, maintaining eye contact, speaking skills, use of fact-finding questions, time management and awareness of personal strengths and weaknesses.

By breaking down a problem situation into manageable "bite size" pieces, the Life Skills students can identify the skills in which they have competence and the skills which could be enhanced in order to solve that situation better.

Start w/ Stimulus.

Rationale Goals	Reasons for the lesson preparation make group aware of coach's agenda
Stimulus	Problem or situation presented to stimulate feelings amongst group members
Evocation	Students respond with feelings and opinions to the stimulus
Objective Enquiry	Students share/learn resources and theory related to the presented problem
Skills Practise	Students practise behaviours/skills learned in the objective enquiry
Application	Students transfer skills to real-life situations
Evaluation	Students/coach assess learning and achievement of goals

Figure 5 Phases at a Glance

Methodology

Structure of the Life Skills Lesson

Although the sequence of lessons may vary and group members help determine content, there is a very definite structure to the

Life Skills lesson. This structure helps differentiate Life Skills training from other models of learning.

Rationale

For each lesson presented, coaches must have a rationale, which can be shared with the group. It is critical that the lesson pertain to the identified needs of the group

Goals

The goals for the lesson are always shared with the group prior to the start of the lesson. They must be behavioural and achievable. The goals can be presented both in a visual and auditory manner. The intent is allow coaches to present the topic for their intended lesson, without a hidden agenda. Success of the lesson does not rely on the achievement of the goals. Needs may arise from the group that supersede the prepared lesson plan.

Phases of the Life Skills Lesson

Stimulus

The Life Skills coach introduces the problem, topic or skill. Various tools or media can be used to stimulate feelings and thoughts in students. For example, a question can be posed, a video shown, a cartoon distributed, a stimulus exercise done.

Evocation

The coach invites students to share their feeling reaction to the stimulus and then their subjective thoughts.

Objective Enquiry

This is the cognitive part of the lesson. The coach and students share outside information and identify potential solutions. Members are asked to shift from their subjective responses (to the stimulus) to a more broad, general or objective approach to the topic. The topic is seen in a larger context, within and outside the group experience. The skills are learned cognitively in this phase.

Skills Practise

The coach provides an opportunity, often through a structured exercise or role play, for students to practise the skill(s). Feedback and processing of the experience is encouraged. This phase helps to ensure integration and assimilation of the learning.

Application

As a result of their learning, students set goals for themselves regarding changes they would like to make in their personal lives. Transferability of skills is essential.

Evaluation

Students and coach evaluate their experiences of the lesson. Members identify their personal learning. Personal insight and increased self-awareness are supported and promoted. Students evaluate whether the lesson goals have been achieved.

Accomplishing the coach's goals at the expense of the demonstrated needs of the group is not in keeping with the tenets of the Life Skills philosophy.

3.5   Life Skills Process

Students start at their present level or style of behaviour, set their own goals and increase their array of effective behaviours.
The student:

- accepts training

- commits to the group

- identifies goals/skills

- observes the demonstration of skill(s)

- practises new skill(s) in the group

- discusses the practice of skill (feedback)

- practises new skill outside of group in personal life

- evaluates the skill back in group

- uses the skills after the completion of the course

- integrates the skills, by teaching new skills to others

Transfer of Skills

The Life Skills course attempts to aid students to become aware of creative problem-solving processes and practise them. Then, when they are integrated at the level of unconscious competence, the new creative behaviour become part of the students automatic responses to problem situations. The criterion for success in meeting the Life Skills program objectives is the continuation of the Life Skills integration process in an individual after training has ceased. The student becomes a self-directed learner.

Unlike many educational programs which assume transfer of learning or leave it to the student to apply the learning, success of the Life Skills course requires that individuals make effective transfer of their problem-solving skills within and outside of group (see Figure 6)[5].

The Life Skills course is successful if learners demonstrate both the ability to practise the skills in group, use the skills in their personal lives and teach these skills to others in their life situation.

This method of skills acquisition abbreviated as P U T:
  Practise
  Use
  Teach
is the measure by which Life Skills integration can be evaluated as being successful.

---

[5]Ralph Himsl, Life Skills: A Course in Applied Problem Solving, in *Readings in Life Skills*, (Prince Albert, Saskatchewan: Saskatchewan NewStart and Training Research and Development Station, 1973), p. 24.

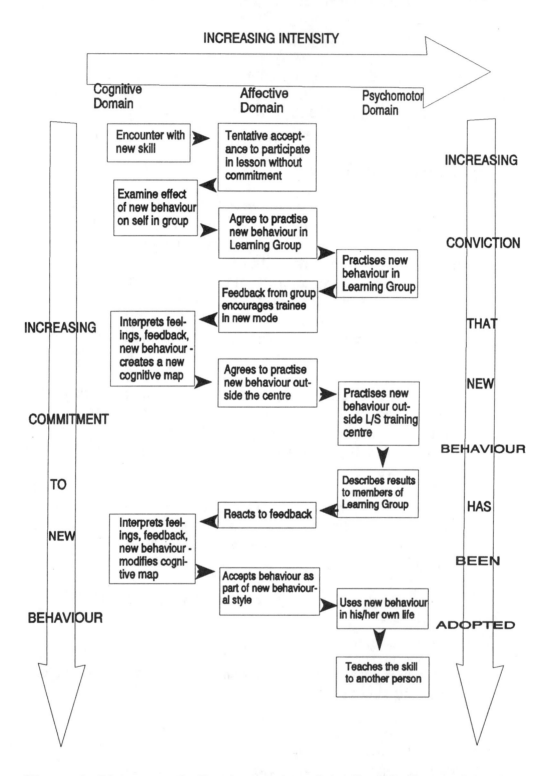

Figure 6 Diagrammatic Representation of the Development of the Skill Transfer Process

Student Response to The Process Dimensions of Life Skills

The Life Skills course integrates content and three process dimensions: a student response to content dimension (Figure 7), a student use of group dimension (Figure 7) and a problem-solving dimension (Figure 8).

Student Response to Content Dimension

In responding along this dimension, participants may react first in any one of the three domains: cognitive, affective or psychomotor. The combination of the affective, cognitive and psychomotor domains in the learning process is known as confluence.

When students react in the cognitive or knowing domain, they might for example, rephrase a sentence in their own words. Or they might summarize what happens in a lesson; if so, they might combine the rather simple act of recalling, with the more complex act of synthesizing. Or they might relate the discussion in a lesson to a personal life experience, thereby showing relationships. Any management of course content such as repetition or recall, explanation, analysis, application, synthesis or evaluation represents a cognitive or knowing response.

Students may also respond on another dimension with affect or feelings. This affective response can occur before, at the same time or after the cognitive or knowing response. Whatever the exact sequence, the Life Skills course recognizes the affective reaction and the coach encourages its expression and management. The coach gives direct assistance and models in the expression of feelings. At worst, unexpressed or suppressed feelings inhibit the development of behavioral change and prevent students from facing themselves and others. At best, expressed feelings open participants to a new understanding of those around them, helping them recognize that others have the same fears and uncertainties they have and yet manage to function in spite of them.

When the students respond in the third domain, the psychomotor or acting category, they use their bodies. They may move about as required in trust exercises, go onto the street to conduct interviews, go with a group on excursions, demonstrate new behaviour to others or participate in role-playing situations. The participants' psychomotor responses often provide the most obvious evidence of their full participation in the activities of the lesson. Their cognitive or knowing management of the content provides them with a necessary factual base; their affective or feeling response to content expresses their willingness to face the consequences of the new knowledge and its effect on them; their psychomotor response represents their commitment to action.

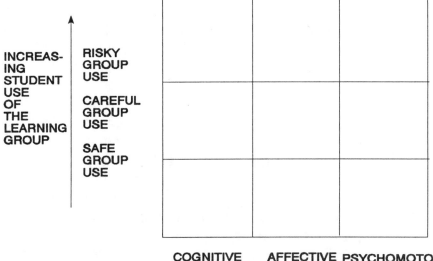

INCREAS-
ING
STUDENT
USE
OF
THE
LEARNING
GROUP

RISKY
GROUP
USE

CAREFUL
GROUP
USE

SAFE
GROUP
USE

COGNITIVE   AFFECTIVE   PSYCHOMOTOR
(Knowing)   (Feeling)   (Acting)
STUDENT RESPONSE TO CONTENT

Figure 7 The Dimensions of Student Response to Content and Use of the Learning Group

The Student Use of Group Dimension

The student use of group dimension describes the purpose of the learning group. The learners use the group to practice new behaviour. They use feedback from the group to modify behaviour and they use the group as a setting in which to develop skills of self-expression. The group affects its members most when members have developed a strong sense of mutual trust and an interest in helping each other through the lessons.

The group provides both acceptance and challenge. Total acceptance may make everyone feel good, but can inhibit improvement in skills and development of problem-solving capabilities. Total challenge makes people react defensively. It is essential to establish a balance between the two.

Problem-Solving Dimension

The learner can use both the knowledge and student use of group dimensions to their fullest and still achieve none of the objectives of the Life Skills course. The complete Life Skills Process/Content Model requires a third dimension - a wide array of problem-solving behaviours.

An individual:

- recognizes a problem situation

- defines the problem

- generates possible solutions and predict results

- chooses solutions

- implements the solutions

- evaluates the results

These are the six steps of the problem-solving model, which is discussed in Unit 4.

Of course, each of these processes contains many sub-processes. As participants develop in the Life Skills course, they increase the array of problem-solving behaviours they utilize until, ideally, they call upon these generic skills as the situation requires.

In summary, as the students use the dimensions of the Life Skills process to manage course content, they respond with understanding from the cognitive domain. They also react emotionally in the affective domain. Behaviourally, learners respond in the psychomotor domain through their actions. Finally, using the group to refine their responses to content, students apply an increasing array of problem-solving skills to the situations presented.

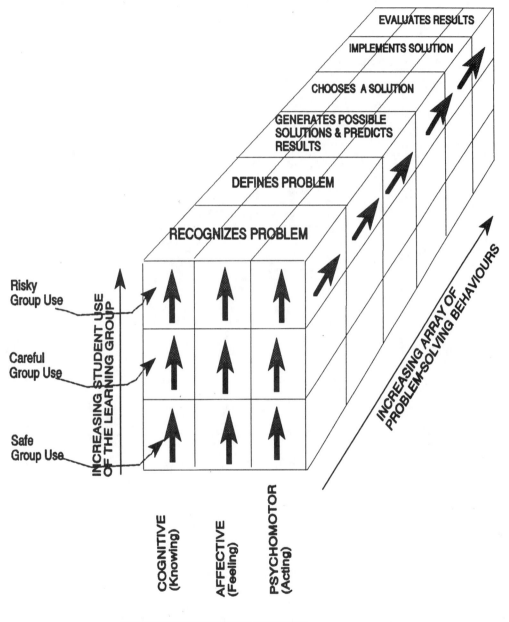

Figure 8 The Life Skills Process Model

4

Creative Problem-Solving Skills

Creative thinking may simply mean the realization that there's no particular virtue in doing things the way they've always been done.
Roger Van Oech

4.1 Problem-Solving as a System

While various authors have described methods of creative problem-solving (CPS) differing in the strategies and language used, there is general agreement that effective CPS follows a sequence of phases. Many systems were designed to facilitate problem-solving in industry, technology, science and mathematics. The model used in the Life Skills course was adapted and designed to teach CPS skills to students wanting to manage their everyday life problems.

This model is based on the assumption that specific behaviour and strategies can be learned to help participants become more creative in their problem-solving activities. Problem-solving involves an interplay of basic skills learned separately, yet used in combination, as part of a larger process. A baseball analogy has been used to suggest that problem-solving is not a lock-step process but rather one that draws together several skills in varying sequences depending on the situation:

Learning to solve problems is like learning to play baseball. You learn to throw, to catch, to bat, to run base, to make plays and to execute all sorts of refinements of these basic skills. You learn these basic skills separately and you put them together in new combinations every game...there is no one-two-three method for solving problems. You learn the skills and you combine them to play the game as circumstances dictate[1].

While there are steps to follow in the problem-solving model, there should also be room to re-visit earlier steps if a solution is not forthcoming (see Figure 11).

Solve is not the ideal word to use in discussing life problems because it implies the same clarity and finality of mathematical problem-solving. Rather, in dealing with personal or interpersonal issues, a problem can be considered solved when a person feels relief, satisfaction or a sense of resolve even if it is not necessarily a perfect solution.

A personal problem can be considered solved when:

• discomfort is reduced to an acceptable level

• an individual is content with the path taken

• the situation has improved

In fact, in most cases, the word *resolve* is a more appropriate concept than *solve*. While resolve involves reducing the state of conflict, restlessness and discomfort, a problem can change even as it is being dealt with or studied.

Creative problem-solving is a dynamic process involving a constant shift of thinking. When a problem is approached from different perspectives, problem solvers may find that each direction may have opposite, yet equally valid or useful considerations. Without an agreed upon orderly process, solving problems may be like trying to hold on to a slippery eel.

Solving problems:

• creates order

---

[1]E. Hodnett, *The Art of Problem Solving: How To Improve Your Methods* (New York: Harper and Row, 1955). Quoted in Dynamics of Life Skills Coaching, 1973, p. 87.

- reduces anxiety, fear, concern

- works best if approached in an organized way

- involves divergent (creative, intuitive) and convergent (linear, logical and selective) thinking processes

Resolutions:

- are rarely the only answer

- are simply the best, given the circumstances

Learning a New Skill

Problem-solving can be thought of in terms of learning. It is one type of learning which, from the perspective of the learner, also follows a sequential process. For example, the following stages are typically experienced when individuals are learning a new skill:

- Unconscious incompetence:
  Learners are not skilled and do not realize it.
  This might be called the *ignorance is bliss* stage.

- Conscious incompetence:
  Competencies are not yet integrated. Learners are acutely aware that skills are still lacking.
  This stage can be very frustrating and acting out behaviours are common.

- Conscious competence:
  Individuals still feel somewhat self-conscious while practising the new behaviour.
  However, they are aware that they are improving their skills and getting more proficient.

- Unconscious competence:
  Skills are now integrated and a natural part of how individuals behave.
  To others, it looks so easy and seamless.

Individual Problem-Solving Styles

In the same way that people have different learning styles and temperaments, so too do they have a problem-solving style they feel most comfortable using. More precisely, different phases of the problem-solving process will appeal to participants because of their preferences and temperaments. Some make decisions very quickly while others take a long time. Some are driven by the emotions generated in the process; others are caught up in brainstorming ideas or in the logical orderly systematic way of proceeding.

For example, styles could be classified as:

- direct and action-oriented

- reflective

- emotional (drawing on feelings and personal data)

- conceptual (open to ideas and factual data)

- methodical

There is no right or wrong style. What is important is that participants understand their particular style and appreciate that not everyone approaches the task of problem-solving the same way as they do. More importantly, it is the situation which dictates the most appropriate style.

For example, in a crisis situation, the *direct* approach might be a more appropriate and responsible style than a reflective one. However, a more *reflective* style might be more appropriate if a person is planning a career change and not quite sure how to proceed.

In fact, the ideal situation is one in which the participants measure their approach relative to the phase, task or situation at hand despite their automatic, preferred way to handle it. This point is central in Life Skills and is captured in the definition, quoted throughout this text, namely, that Life Skills are problem-solving behaviours used <u>appropriately</u> and <u>responsibly</u> in the management of everyday affairs.

The goal of the Life Skills program is to expose students to all the problem-solving behaviours listed throughout this section in order to expand their repertoire of skills in all areas of life.

Human Relations and Problem-Solving

It could be said that human relations or interpersonal skills are one type of problem-solving. Although the behaviours involved in CPS are performed by an individual, the context of these behaviours usually involves other people. This situation is especially true in Life Skills courses designed to develop learners' problem-solving abilities. In fact, learning to solve problems appropriately and responsibly as group members is a raison d'être of Life Skills programs.

Figure 8 conceptualizes the *Life Skills Process Model*. It shows how groups move from safe to riskier ways of relating to one another. In Life Skills groups, participants are learning to develop human relations or interpersonal skills in three learning domains, namely, cognitive (head), affective (heart) and psychomotor (body), while practising thinking and problem-solving skills as part of the group process.

Group process refers to the experience of learning and working together as a group. Put differently, learners are immediately applying what is being learned, namely, interpersonal, critical thinking and problem-solving skills both within and outside the group.

The expression, "the process is the content" which characterizes the Life Skills philosophy and methodology is very evident when groups are learning to problem-solve together. Here participants are practising fact-finding, critical thinking, observation, creativity, conflict resolution, communication skills and BSD behaviours as they work together to solve problems. Practising, using, teaching (PUT) what is being learned is a key concept in Life Skills programs. This way of teaching/learning is also referred to as the Life Skills experiential learning model.

Life Skills involve CPS where the person deals with both events and people in various situations. Because life offers daily challenges, individuals are constantly learning new skills to deal with them.

At times, an individual has control of some elements of the problem and can manipulate these like pieces in a jigsaw puzzle. However, life problems almost always involve other people. Because several people are involved with the problem, it does not hold still like a puzzle. Thus, in solving problems, people need to develop skills that help them relate to one another effectively as well as those that help them deal with ever-changing elements of the problems.

In the Life Skills context:

- problem-solving skills refer to behaviour aimed at producing a desired change

- human relations skills refer to behaviour which improves interaction so that interpersonal conflicts do not interfere with efforts to solve problems

Decision-Making and Goal-Setting

Decision-making and goal setting are also problem-solving activities. Human relations behaviour involves encountering personal values and often ends up as a problem-solving process out of which comes a decision. Goal-setting as a form of decision-making is therefore another life skill intimately linked to problem-solving.

Effective decision-making requires constant re-examination of goals set and made. When additional information or new experiences indicate that change would be more desirable than the status quo, people may re-visit their goals and decisions and make modifications. This is in fact, a problem-solving process.

At the human relations level, Life Skills students learn to work interdependently, handle issues, make decisions, set goals, communicate with one another all in an appropriate and responsible manner. *Appropriate and responsible*, as stated earlier in the definition of Life Skills, mean that they critically reflect upon issues in light of the larger context, stages of the group, their needs and needs of the others. Once assessed, they then act accordingly.

For example, effective problem-solvers:

- understand and implement skills required to solve the problem

- understand their roles, know why they are in these roles and can explain the significance of their behaviour

- ask questions beginning with "in what ways might...?" to help define the problem

- identify assumptions by asking "why"

- can perform a variety of behaviour if required; do not get locked into a limited number of roles in the group

- know how to gather facts to help define a problem

- learn problem-solving to put together pieces of a puzzle and human relations skills to resolve conflicts which might arise in solving problems with others

- apply both sets of skills (human relations and problem-solving) to effect change in order to meet their goals

- practise problem-solving in both real and simulated situations in Life Skills courses; have learned to transfer learning from one context to another

4.2 Problem-Solving in Life Skills

The Life Skills Problem-Solving System

While it is possible to describe CPS in a systematic, step-by-step method, most people do not go through such a formalized process. Most behaviour is automatic. The map is not the territory, but a map is nevertheless helpful. In this case, the map is the six step problem-solving system.

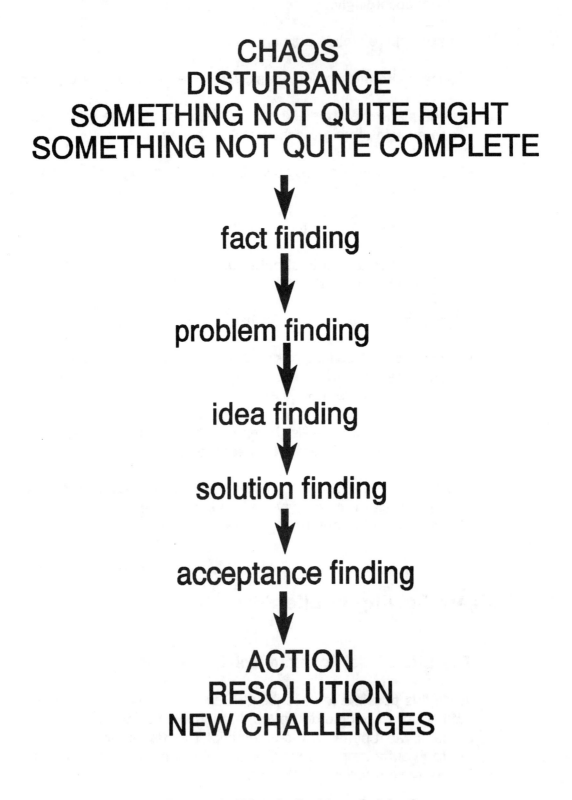

Figure 9 What is Problem-Solving?

The Life Skills course attempts to help trainees become more aware of problem-solving processes and to practise them in a formalized way. Then, when they are integrated at the level of "unconscious competence", this new, creative behaviour become part of the students' automatic responses to problem situations. The following discussion and illustration outline various ways to consider the Life Skills six step model.

The Life Skills Six-Step Model

1. Recognize a Problem
   When there is a feeling of discomfort, disturbance, chaos, a problem or challenge is recognized. Until individuals recognize there is a specific problem, the problem-solving process cannot begin.

2. Describe and Define the Problem
   Some individuals begin solving problems without being clear about the issue to be solved. Describing and defining the problem involves using the 5WHs (what, who, where, when, why and how) system to gather more facts before beginning to consider ways of dealing with the problem.
   "Why" questions which can be too "leading" are deferred until the second half of this step as a way to test assumptions.

3. Generate Ideas
   People often move directly to this step, bypassing the previous two. This can result in unsuccessful problem-solving. Once the problem has been defined in terms of its priority, level of seriousness and whose problem it is, individuals or groups can move on to considering alternative ways of dealing with it. Tried and true suggestions as well as outrageous ideas are entertained at this stage. Brainstorming is a technique used to encourage less obvious solutions. Judgements and critiques are withheld at this point so that the creative juices can flow without censor. This process requires divergent, creative thinking people.

4. Make a Decision
   Choosing from alternatives and committing to the best available alternative, involves convergent thinking. Typically, individuals or groups list, then prioritize criteria to help them choose a solution. Criteria could be things like accessibility,

cost, time, resources, values or philosophy.

An excellent tool to use at this stage is the Force-field analysis developed by Kurt Lewin. (See Figure 12) Here individuals list forces that could help them to realize the goal and those that could hinder or need to be overcome. A further step is an analysis of ways the positive factors could be enhanced and the negative factors eliminated or minimized. This process both analyzes the issues and creates a plan of action. This step involves both divergent and convergent thinking processes.

5. Implement the Decision
Making a decision to deal with the problem involves designing an action plan, finding a way to evaluate its success, anticipating new problems and putting the plan in action.

6. Evaluation
At this stage after the plan has been implemented, the individual or group de-briefs in detail and assesses what happened. They determine whether it was a success or not, how they felt about the process, the outcome and whether there is another problem to solve. This often happens in subsequent sessions.

If the problem was resolved, they will want to reflect on the process in order to learn from it. If there was no resolution, they will want to identify the difficulties at each stage and perhaps re-state the problem, review the ideas listed or generate new approaches to the problem.

1. <u>Recognize a Problem</u>:
   - feel disappointed, restless or the expectations not met
   - sense something is not right or needs to change
   - become aware there is a task to do

2. <u>Describe and Define the Problem</u>:
   - gather facts 5WH (what, where, when, why and how)
   - ask questions such as: "in what ways might...?"
   - test each "in what ways might...?" questions with a "why?" to discover assumptions
   - establish problem ownership
   - agree on the definition of one problem
   - thinking is divergent and convergent

3. <u>Generate Ideas</u>:
   - brainstorm ways of dealing with the problem
   - withhold judgments
   - thinking is divergent

4. <u>Make a Decision</u>:
   - list criteria to help choose and prioritize solution
   - analyze factors (force-field analysis)
   - choose from alternatives
   - create an action plan
   - thinking is convergent and divergent

5. <u>Implement the Decision</u>:
   - implement an action plan
   - find a way to evaluate success
   - anticipate new problems

6. <u>Evaluation</u>:
   - de-brief and assess
   - determine if it was a success or not and what was learned
   - compare results with predictions and expectations
   - re-define problem, or generate new ideas, if necessary
   - identify any new problems to solve

Figure 10 The Life Skills Problem-Solving System

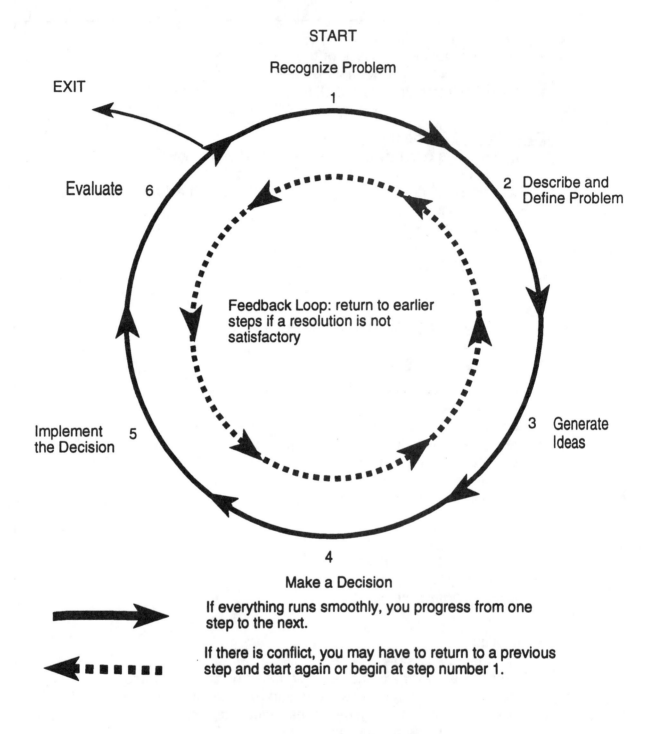

Figure 11 The Life Skills Six-Step Problem-Solving System

SUPPORTS+   BARRIERS-

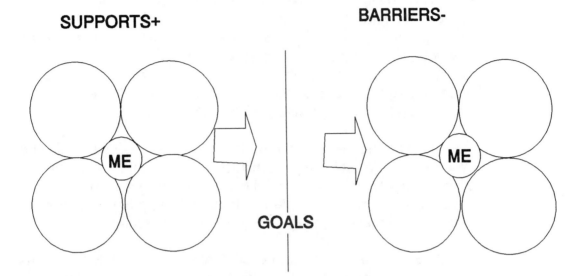

GOALS

Examine your supports and barriers
Which additional resources are necessary to get to your goal?

ADDITIONAL RESOURCES NEEDED

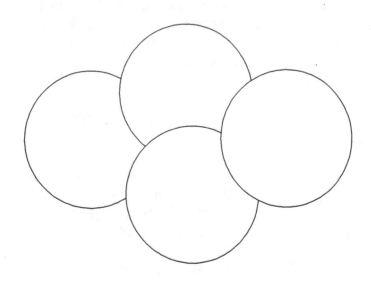

Figure 12 Force-Field Analysis

The Concept of Pulsating Thinking

In working through the Creative Problem-Solving (CPS) phases, there is a constant shift from a divergent to convergent approaches known as "pulsating thinking". Applying the "pulsating thinking" concept, the six CPS phases show that problem-solving has both a sequential and back and forth flow. The term, "feedback loop" refers to the idea that feedback given and heard at each stage might influence the problem-solvers to re-visit earlier stages to review their process and ideas.

Recognizing and defining the problem involves divergent thinking. When there is a tentative commitment to one definition of the problem, the members have shifted to convergent thinking. In developing as many possible solutions to the problem as possible in the idea-generating stage, they return to divergent thinking.

Deciding to include or reject possible alternative solutions returns to convergent thinking. If it is difficult to discover alternatives, a re-definition of the problem and a return to phase one may be necessary (feedback loop). Considering possible implications for action of each alternative takes them back to divergent thinking. When they make a decision and commit to a course of action, they are in a convergent thinking mode.

If none of the alternatives seem suitable or the decision proves inadequate, it is important to return to earlier steps either to re-conceptualize the problem, re-examine alternatives or to develop new alternatives (feedback loop).

Translating Theory Into Practice

The major steps in the Life Skills problem-solving model are: recognition of a problem, definition of a problem, generating ideas, choosing and implementing a solution and evaluating the result. These steps provide some definition of the problem-solving process, but the words are too abstract to translate into behaviour. What are people really doing when defining a problem? What people actually do in defining a problem differs from one situation to another even though the same term describes what they each intend to do.

In defining a problem, for example, one person states what she wants to achieve (*I need a change; I want to paint the apartment dark green!*); another person names the obstacles (*I'll never get that landlord to agree if I tell him what colour I want to paint my apartment*); another summarizes what bothers him (*I haven't got enough money to paint this myself*). Individuals have their own way of looking at the problem which will lead them to different ways of defining and dealing with it. Person one has foreclosed any discussion on other ways to "have a change" by focusing on painting; person two will be focusing on how to deal with the landlord; person three will be working on finding money.

On the other hand, Life Skills students who have been taught the six step method have learned to use "in what ways might...?" questions as a common technique to help define the problem. These questions provide a search device for generating ideas as well as defining the problem. This tool combines two strategies in one operation, for example, *In what ways might I change my environment?*

Words such as *define* and *identify* are abstractions of processes, labels for strategies or intentions or explanations of behaviour not prescriptions for action. Even though people recognize the difference between abstract labels and the actual behaviour, there is another problem when individuals try to match experience with theoretical concepts. How does the group know when someone is defining a problem? What does it look like?

When people ask a question starting with the words, "in what ways might...?" are they necessarily defining the problem? Might they be actually seeking alternative solutions? Are they effectively defining a problem if they do not understand the relationship between their behaviour and their unconscious intention? Are they merely parroting a response they know the coach wants?

One of the tasks of the Life Skills coach involves understanding the relationship between theory and practice, translating abstract directives into specific, observable behavioural operations and modelling those operations.

The theory underlying Life Skills includes the following three dimensions: human relations skills, problem-solving skills and thinking skills. These skills are all inter-related and students bring them to bear on their life problems. However, description of the theory is quite abstract; it only provides a framework for understanding how different behaviours fit together and how they can result in creative problem-solving.

Abstract labels must be translated into specific behaviour in order to practise and get feedback on creative problem-solving skills. However, behavioural descriptions lose meaning if removed from the theoretical framework to which they refer. The meaning is contained in the interpretation given to the process, not in the behaviour itself.

Because the behaviour descriptions consist of observable behaviour such as "look at", "lean forward", "listen", they can also be interpreted differently depending on their context. Listening to an authority figure versus listening to a student may have quite different meanings even though the behaviour (listening) is the same. Thus, behaviour has no meaning or explanatory power outside of its theoretical framework or context.

This then, is the rationale behind the importance of theory in the practice of Life Skills. Every Life Skills lesson needs to have both an objective enquiry or theoretical context, as well as opportunity to practise the skills being discussed.

Some Behaviours Used in Creative Problem-Solving

The following list provides a start for identifying skills used at various points in a problem-solving process:

- asking questions (for information or clarification)
- categorizing
- comparing
- contracting
- challenging assumptions
- critiquing
- deferring judgement
- defining
- describing (feelings)
- evaluating (consequences)
- fantasizing
- generalizing
- giving and receiving feedback

- identifying (problems, needs)
- interpreting and checking meanings
- interviewing
- juxtaposing
- listening
- listing
- measuring
- naming
- organizing (information)
- paraphrasing
- planning
- predicting
- predicting outcomes
- rank ordering (criteria)
- rating
- reading
- recording data
- reporting
- seeking and examining assumptions
- sequencing
- setting goals
- summarizing
- tabulating
- using logic
- watching

The preceding list of skills used in the various problem-solving phases and processes is not complete and should be added to as one becomes familiar with the Life Skills problem-solving system. Any one skill is not confined to one phase of problem-solving. It can be used in several phases. Throughout a Life Skills course, participants explore a wide variety of behaviours which enhance their CPS skills.

Applying Problem-Solving in Groups

Solving problems requires information, ideas and different ways of looking at and approaching a problem. If a problem involves other people, as most problems do, it helps to work with others. Different people see different ways to approach the problem. In other words, more heads are better than one.

Since people have had different life experiences in dealing with problems, the group can become a rich resource to draw on when looking for alternative ways to deal with a problem. Working together, a group can share different feelings, viewpoints and information. Together they can consider a number of ways to deal with the problem.

If the problem affects only one person, the group problem-solving process helps to expand an individual's repertoire of choices. The individual can then choose how to deal with it.

Not all groups are problem-solving groups. It takes skill and practice for people to work well together. Most groups need to practise helpful group behaviour. The sections on group dynamics, interpersonal skills and BSD behaviour discussed in other units describe this behaviour. Life Skills lessons such as those outlined in the YWCA of Metropolitan Toronto manuals, *Discovering Life Skills, Volumes I-VII*[2], give groups ample opportunity to practise them.

Facilitating a Discussion About Problem-Solving

As well as experiencing problem-solving exercises, groups will discover that some methods work better than others, depending on the problem. The following questions can be asked to help members to classify different approaches once each method has been reviewed. For example, the facilitator may ask the following questions:

- Which type of problem-solving method do you typically use at work? at home?

- Why might there be a difference?

- What types of problems are best solved by logical processes?

- What types of problems are best solved by lateral thinking and free association methods?

---

[2]*Discovering Life Skills, Volumes I-VII*, (Toronto: YWCA of Metropolitan Toronto, 1976-1995).

• When would a combination of the two be appropriate?

Examples of Problem-Solving at Different Stages of the Process

While groups often solve problems just by sharing ideas, it can help to have a systematic way to go about approaching a problem. Moving in an orderly way, the group is less likely to overlook an important step. For example, to avoid solving the wrong problem, they can check if they have defined the problem correctly before developing an action plan.

The following examples describe the step-by-step method using sample scenarios which lend themselves to problem-solving in a group:

Step One: Become aware of a problem

Members become aware a problem exists and point this out to the group. There is a sense that things need to improve and change.

Examples

The person who initiates this step might say something like:

A *I am feeling uptight. This group is really tense today. What's bugging everyone?*

B *Luis, you look upset about something. Can we help you in any way?*

C *I'm having problems with my boss and I would like to get some help from you people.*

None of these statements specifies what the problem is; they however, indicate that there is a problem and the group might be able to help them look at and solve it. If the group has indicated its willingness to work on this issue, the next task is to define the problem.

Step Two: Define the problem

Some agreement on the definition of the problem must be reached, since ideas cannot be generated until this is known. By having the group think and talk about the problem, different ways of looking at it are expressed. Different aspects are brought out so that all members get a better understanding. Clarity of the problem is key.

The group has to agree on the <u>main</u> problem. Some members may see other related or lesser problems, but to proceed with the problem-solving process, the group must agree to deal with one problem. This problem-solving process works if groups deal with one problem at a time.

This step can be the most time consuming. It is well worth it to take time to check that all agree before proceeding to the next step. By doing a thorough job of defining the problem, it may be already half-solved.

During this phase, the group:

• talks about the problem

• identifies the causes

• gathers and organizes information

• identifies the assumptions being made

• stops blaming others as the cause

• gets more information

• assesses degree of seriousness

• decides how extensive the problem is

• determines how many people are affected

• sets limits on the problem to manage it

• sets aside other related problems for another discussion

- defines problem in a written form

- makes certain that all members understand and agree on what the problem is

Examples

To start this phase of the problem-solving process, the following might be said:

A *I think that one reason why the group is so tense is that we are getting a different coach Monday and nobody is sure what's going to happen.*

B *Luis may say, "My kid is starting to hang out with a bunch of druggies and I'm afraid he might land in jail. How do you talk sense into kids nowadays?"*

C *The group will ask, "Give us some examples of the kind of trouble you are having with your boss."*

These examples illustrate the beginnings of the definition of the problem. When the group has decided what the problem is they go on to step three.

Step Three A: Produce ideas, solutions, facts related to the problem

Having agreed upon the problem to be solved, the group begins to produce ideas about it. The objective is to get as many ideas as possible without judgements. Members do not worry about how good the ideas are at this time. The ideas generated build up until they begin to form possible solutions. A stepping-stone metaphor is used to encourage members to offer outrageous ideas because they may act as a stepping stone for someone else's idea otherwise not considered. Each member is encouraged to speak.

Before arriving at the final part of this step (producing a list of possible solutions) the group records as many possible causes of the problem.

During this phase, the group:

- thinks up and records many causes and ideas

- seeks out and relates new knowledge to the problem

- gathers information and facts

- becomes aware of difference of opinions, unanswered questions

- may redefine the problem

Examples

A *One way we could help the group adjust to a new coach is to have both coaches with us for a few days next week.*

B *Luis, I heard about a tape made by a kid whose best friend died strung out on speed. The kids who heard it on the radio were shaken up by it. Maybe this might jolt your son and his friends?*

C *Sounds like you have no power or influence in this situation with your boss. Why don't you take him out for dinner?*

As the examples show, in this phase ideas are not judged or criticized because the purpose is just to produce them.
Each one must be examined critically or "tested against reality" in the next step.

Step Three B: Examine the ideas critically

Reality-testing the ideas means deciding whether or not they are relevant and practical. It also means making predictions about what would happen if the solutions were implemented.

Further information might be required regarding some of the suggestions. Members may need to do some homework if the group does not have all the information at that point. Such things as human rights, laws, regulations, available programs, services will have to be investigated.

Implications of certain solutions may rule them out on a

preliminary examination. Facts are gathered which have a bearing on the remaining solutions until there is an adequate basis for decision. Three criteria for testing a proposed solution might be: (1) in what way does it help solve the problem? (2) can it be put into practise? (3) will there be undesirable side effects created by the solution?

During this phase, the individual with the problem:

- examines the ideas critically for relevance

- determines the implications of each solution

- if necessary, gathers more information and facts

- shares feelings, biases and opinions about the ideas

- draws on the experiences and knowledge of group members

- lists and analyzes points "for and against" the proposals

Examples

A *How do you (coach) feel about having two coaches in the group for a few days until we get used to the change? Are you free to stay with us a few more days?*

B *Does anyone know where to get that tape? I understand it was aired on CBC. How does one get stuff from the CBC?*

C *I'm not interested in taking the boss for dinner. I want him to take me seriously at work.*

After the group has seriously considered ideas as solutions, eliminated others, combined groupings into similar categories, predicated outcomes and consequences, created for and against points for each, it should be ready to move on to the next sub-step of choosing one to act on.

Step Three C: Select the best solution

The group should then try to come to a consensus on the best solution to the problem. At this point, the group has defined the problem; produced possible solutions and "reality tested" them; listed the proposed solutions showing the favourable and unfavourable features of each one. The group then selects the best solutions from the list. If the problem applies only to one or two members of the group, the individuals directly involved must necessarily have the final say as to what they are going to do. The group, however, seeks a commitment from these members to put one solution into action and they may use their knowledge and skills to help these members reach a "best" solution. Sometimes one solution stands out from the rest and sometimes not. Sometimes at this stage, the better parts of two or more solutions may be combined. Often, the solution is actually a complex plan of action requiring many sub-solutions. Frequently, life being what it is, there may be no really satisfying solution and the group must be content with the best of several mediocre solutions.

Finally, the group re-examines the implications of the selected solution, looks to see what might happen if the solution is implemented and tries to predict outcomes. The group members must feel confident that the solution will be practical to use. If for some reason the solution does not seem right, the group should consider another solution. Whether the members with the problem decide by themselves or use the other members of the group to help them come to a consensus on the "best" solution, some type of decision is necessary in order to make a detailed plan for action and to put the solution into practise in the next step.

Examples

A *Have we all agreed then that we will have both coaches for Monday and Tuesday next week so that we can work on this problem of changing coaches? Is there anyone who is unhappy with this solution?*

B *Luis, will you get together with your son and his friends with this video tape? Maybe it won't do any good but how could it hurt? We would like a commitment from you that you won't complain about how much trouble you have with him without trying something. Will you agree to try showing him the tape?*

C *Since I can't quit my job, I've just got to live with this crummy boss. Figuring out how to keep him happy is a*

good solution and you have given me some good ideas,
so let's work out some plans for doing it.

Step Four A: Plan the action in detail

The proposed action needs to be thought through in as much detail as is considered necessary by the group or individuals involved - how it may be done and the implications. When the group members are satisfied that they are moving in the right direction, they make a detailed plan for action. This action plan is then judged for its relevance and whether it will in fact, solve the problem. It is also judged for its practicality. If there is any doubt whether the plan will work, the group will want to do some replanning to make it more relevant to the problem or more practical to put into effect. During any replanning process, the group will want to return to Step Three and reconsider solutions that were produced. In fact, while planning for action, the group may want to refer to other earlier steps also.

Examples

A   *The first thing to do is see if we can get the training supervisor to free up the coaches' time on Monday. Then we can make more detailed plans on how we're going to handle the problem of changing coaches.*

B   *We know where to get a copy of the tape. Now we need to plan how to get this kid and his friends to listen. The group feels that the best approach is to have the tape on at the party. We need to plan this party and where the best point would be to play the tape.*

C   *What can you do to make your boss happy? You said he really likes it when you review the tasks that still need to be done for the next day. Why not keep doing this as a daily practise?*

The above examples illustrate the beginning of the detailed planning. Once the group is reasonably satisfied that they know what they are going to do and feel comfortable about doing it, then they must DO IT. That is next step.

Step Four B: Do it

Acting on the plan is an essential step. If the previous steps have been completed in sufficient detail, carrying out the plan should be relatively easy. It does require courage and mutual support; if the group is working as an effective Life Skills group, this support will be available. If no action is taken and no change in behaviour occurs, then much of the work in previous steps has been misguided, unless the problem was resolved by its clarification. This is a possible outcome if the problem was caused by confusion or lack of information. People may change their behaviour if they have gained a different viewpoint on the issue. It is important to keep in mind that an analysis of a problem will imply some action or course of action which must be taken if the problem is to be handled.

Step Five: Evaluate the outcome of the action

In order to learn from experience, members must think about the experience. In evaluating the outcome of a plan, what happened is compared with what was predicted. The evaluation should include a statement of how well the action helped solve the problem; how the plan that was formulated compared with the actual action taken; which aspects of the plan were accurate forecasts and which ones were not.

New problems can arise out of the solutions (actions) to the old ones. Individuals may need to redefine the problem or define a new facet of the old problem. Rarely do things get solved once and for all. If problem-solving has been successful, at the very least the old problem no longer exists.

Examples

A   *I appreciated hearing them both talk about their ideas about Life Skills. It helped me to learn more about the new coach and even though she will be different, some things will remain the same. I'm not as anxious anymore.*

B   *That tape partially worked. Some of the kids got mad and some started talking about their use of dope. My kid was mad at me for playing the tape at the party and we had a big fight about it afterward but I think it got to him.*

C *My boss really loves the way I am reporting in each day, outlining my tasks and ending each day with what will be done the next day. You were right in saying that I should appeal to his "true colour" needs. It's no big deal for me and yet it means a lot to him, so why not keep doing it? I've noticed he seems to take me more seriously as a result.*

These examples are the beginning of the evaluation stage. The group compares the plans with what was actually done and finds out what worked, what didn't and why. What should have been done differently? Could they have planned for it in a better way? Particular attention should be paid to changes in behaviour before and after the plan was implemented. By using a step-by-step method, members of the group have learned a generic way to solve problems and possible ways to prevent similar problems in the future.

4.3 Samples of Different Problem-Solving Exercises

The following are examples of exercises used in a problem-solving lesson. The first one, *mind mapping* uses free association to identify patterns and issues. It tends to by-pass critical thinking processes. The second exercise called a *suggestion circle*, is used when participants ask the member for feedback regarding a problem they have outside the group. The person has already defined the problem and is now looking for ideas to consider. It uses fact-finding, questioning, information-gathering skills which tend to be more linear to arrive at logical solutions.

The next method called *Dear Ann Landers*, is used when participants want input about a problem they are having but are not ready to self-disclose to the group. The final one called *About Face* also ensures member's need for privacy by having problems and solutions written on pieces of paper which are distributed and discussed anonymously.

The samples show that there are a variety of methods available which will allow participants to have input to their issues openly or anonymously at every stage of the group.

Mind Mapping

Mind mapping is a tool which encourages free association in the brainstorming stage of a problem-solving process. It uses divergent thinking to generate information quickly and spontaneously. This method can net ideas and feelings which might be overlooked using more linear methods. Ideas flow rapidly and in random sequence. Once a personal or group-related issue has been identified, the group may decide to use this method in two ways. It can be used as a group exercise in which someone writes word and phases on the flipchart for everyone to see. Or, members may decide to use the method on an individual basis. In the latter case, they would do their own mind map which can be kept private or shared with others. While the general approach can be decided by the group, the actual steps are to be agreed upon with no deviations.

Steps

- The coach (or individual) writes a key word or phrase in the middle of the flipchart or page and draws a circle around it. (See sample in Figure 13)

- The group (or individual) records any words, phrases, images, symbols that come to mind.

- Participants circle each one and connect these associations to the central word with a line. This group of words and phrases is called a *cluster*.

- Participants then return to the central word and generate a new cluster.

- They continue to develop new strings of word or phrase clusters until all possibilities are exhausted.

- The next step is to write for five minutes non-stop ("five minute sprint") not worrying about spelling and grammar to see what emerges.

- If this is a group problem, participants would share what they have written.

1. Pick one word or phrase for centre

2. Free associate: Generate clusters of words and phrases.

3. Write about for 5 minutes

4. Share with partner or the group, if desirable.

Figure 13 Sample of Mind Mapping

- Suggested topics to be mapped:

  Group related:
  Resistance or conflict
  Goals
  Strengths or areas to improve
  Roles
  Rules

  Personal:
  Managing money
  Changes/Transitions
  Who am I?
  Gaining employment
  Success
  Blue Sky (or dreams)
  Dark Clouds (or fears, worries)
  Feeling empowered

Suggestion Circle

Suggestion circles are used when individuals feel stuck and can not decide what to do next about a situation. It is a very structured approach with definite rules to follow. It is important that the group (especially the person with the problem) agrees to use this particular method. Suggestion circles can empower the group by demonstrating that the wisdom within them can be useful to someone else.

The steps are reviewed so that the group clearly understands the ground rules and boundaries before the process begins. For example, suggestions that advocate violence or abuse are not allowed, even in jest.

Steps

- The person with the problem (A) sits in the front of the group.

- The rest of the group sits around (A) in a circle.

- (A) states the problem in a short sentence.

- The group asks clarifying questions.

- Once (A) has defined the problem and the other members understand the issue, each member writes on index cards concise suggestions for (A) to consider.

- Suggestions are then read aloud one-by-one around the circle in order beginning with the phrase *If this were me, I would (or might)....*

- Participants have the right to pass without being challenged. They simply state, *I pass.*

- (A)'s role is to listen and respond to each member's suggestion with a *Thank you.*

- Others are not to comment or evaluate. They must be stopped if they do so.

- Written suggestions are handed in to (A) to consider on his/her own.

- The process is completed; (A) is not required to make an immediate decision, nor tell the group what s/he plans.

- (A) is encouraged to reflect on what has been said, "sleep on it", make a decision the next day and share the action plan with the group when ready.

- The group may discuss their process without evaluating the ideas.

Anonymous Problem-Solving

In recent formed groups, in groups where safety has not been established or when individuals feel reluctant to self-disclose for a variety of reasons, the six-step problem-solving method may not be the appropriate method to solve specific problems. In these instances anonymous problem-solving methods are available.

Dear Ann Landers

Students write letters to a fictitious problem-solving columnist (Ann Landers or Group Gossip for example) based on personal problems presently being encountered. The letters are signed fictitiously, possibly humourously and collected. Students volunteer to be the problem-solving columnist for one problem. They select a problem randomly, read it aloud and offer possible solutions to the issues. The process continues until all presenting problems have been offered solutions.

About Face

Students anonymously write out problem situations they are currently encountering. These situations are to be written in some depth. The problems are placed in a large envelope.

Participants each receive large piles of small paper squares, in two colours. One colour is identified as the pro, the other as the con colour.

Participants are asked to volunteer to take a turn in choosing, reading aloud and offering solutions to anonymous problem situations. They are told that after they have offered their solutions, other group members will respond to them, symbolically with squares of paper. Group members can offer up to three squares of the pro colour or of the con colour as a symbol of agreement or disagreement with the proposed solution. In cases where members agree (or disagree) in part, combinations of squares can be attributed.

After the symbolic response has been delivered, members are asked to explain the reasons they responded as they did. In this way the anonymous problem-writer will hear a large number of possible responses to a situation, while the focus remains on the volunteer problem-solver.

The process continues until potential solutions to the problems have been presented.

Students are told that this is not a competitive activity and the number of squares collected is not relevant.

5

Group Characteristics and Processes

5.1 Definitions

What are Group Dynamics?

When humans communicate, they are always communicating on two levels: the object or verbal level (the words themselves) and the meta or non-verbal level or interpersonal dynamics. Communication is healthy (even in conflict) when the levels match or are congruent. Ineffective or disturbing communication happens when people are sent mixed messages; meaning, when the levels do not match.

In group dynamics, two levels are also considered when trying to understand what is working or not. Those two levels are referred to as the content and process. The first deals with the subject matter, problem or "task" on which the group is working. The second dimension is concerned with what is happening between members and to the group while it is working. The second level is also referred to as "maintenance" or "relationship" aspects of a group.

What Is a Group?

A group is more than one person. A collection of people becomes a group when members:

- see themselves as a group

- share the same purpose, goals or ideals

- begin to identify with one another

- interact with, influence and react to one another

People belong to many different groups such as the family, work teams, committees, study groups, Life Skills groups. Despite their different tasks, there are certain characteristics, influences and dynamics found in all groups. To determine how a group is working (or not), the following framework which looks at various group dynamics, might be used as a point of reference.

For example, all groups have a history and background which initially and in some cases, consistently influence how they function. To function even more effectively a group might periodically look at <u>how</u> it is functioning in terms of membership and participation issues such as sub-grouping and leadership struggles or communication patterns, group procedures and decision making methods. It might also look at its development, common goals, norms, standards, atmosphere, morale and the degree of cohesiveness that has evolved (or not) in relation to physical, intellectual and emotional needs felt at different stages. Since awareness is fifty percent of the work, the following discussion highlighting each of these aspects can help groups to function effectively.

5.2 Group Development

History and Background

Every Life Skills group has a larger context, history or background which can affect how it functions. For example, if some members of the group already know each other or if some have been mandated to attend the program or if there is continuous intake, additional dynamics are present.

Everyone comes to the group with assumptions, preconceived notions and attitudes. Participants may be uncertain, anxious, curious, indifferent, eager, frightened or puzzled by the group. Participants need to spend time getting to know one another at the beginning to arrive at some commonalties and to minimize any anxious feelings.

Questions to Ask

What forces have brought this group together?

In whose interest was the group originally conceived?

Are members mandated or coming by choice?

Who already knows who?

How are members feeling about being here?

What measures are being used to allow the members to interact with one another?

Membership Issues

In every group, members experience a continuous struggle between SELF and GROUP. Once the initial "best behaviour" stage is over, individual (self) needs generally become dominant. In other words, self needs take precedence over the group's needs, even at the expense of the group.

Only when the individuals' interpersonal needs of inclusion, control, affection (see Figure 14)[1] are met, can the collective needs of the group take precedence. This shift will happen when individuals feel safe and confident that the group will in fact, not

---

[1]William C. Schutz, *Here Comes Everybody* (New York: Harper and Row, 1971), pp. 21-38.

Inclusion Needs

- sense of belonging, being included
- to attract attention and interest of others
- driven by desire to be a member of the group, yet to remain distinct and unique

Control Needs

- for control over others
- to be directed
- are observed as a continuum in the decision-making process
- involve power, authority and influence
- are manifest in a "pecking order" which changes day-to-day

Affection Needs

- to feel close, personal involvement with others
- are expressed by giving and receiving affection
- can be seen in both attraction and aversion between individuals
- can be manifest in friendly behaviour to all or aloof behaviour

Figure 14 Interpersonal Needs in Groups

sabotage their personal needs. Individual needs are then subsumed within the group's needs. Balance between self and group needs can be an ongoing challenge.

Membership can be obtained by:

- sharing common interests and goals

- resolving conflict successfully

- surviving crisis together

- demonstrating commitment to the cause or task (peer pressure or infectious enthusiasm)

Sub-Grouping

Sub-groups develop on the basis of friendships, common interests or shared concerns. Sub-groups form, break up, mix and move around in a healthy group. If sub-groups become fixed, cohesion of the group as a whole can be compromised.

Sometimes sub-groups will resist becoming members because they:

- do not like the direction the large group is taking

- are in a power struggle with the leader or other members

- are not clear what their own needs are

- were mandated to be in the group against their will

Questions to Ask

Are certain members forming cliques?

What effect is this having on the group?

What methods is the coach using to get the group mingling?

Communication and Participation Patterns

A major area of difficulty for a group can be observed in its communication patterns (data flow) and ways of working together.[2] One way to assess the pattern or style of the communication of a group is to analyze it in terms of:

---

[2]For a more in depth discussion on observing groups, see Hedley G. Dimock, *How to Observe Your Group*, Second Edition (Guelph, Ontario: University of Guelph, Centre for Human Development, 1985).

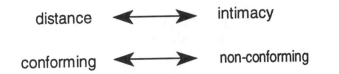

Groups first struggle with the question of how intimate or distant they should be with one another. They also deal with the issue of conformity or non-conformity as the members work at finding the type of communication appropriate for their particular stage of development.

"Conformity" means resolving the question of intimacy and self-versus-group dichotomy. Self-oriented (non-conformist) and distant communication patterns suggest that participants may still be struggling with membership or control issues.

"Intimacy" is the degree to which individuals are willing to get involved personally in the content (or task) and group interactions. When a group is communicating at an intimate level, members have found their place in the group. Healthy communication patterns and styles are determined by the trust and safety levels in the group.

Patterns of participation can be mapped out as sociograms (see Figure 15) to help members understand their lines of communication. Interaction patterns look like webs of influences: coach speaks to the group; participants talk to one another; participants talk to the coach; coach talks to individual participants.

Members may be talking to one another but not necessarily communicating, in the sense of understanding or being understood. Non verbal messages (tones, posture, expressions and gestures) indicate willingness and reluctance speak up.

Questions to Ask

Who is speaking to whom? How often? In what manner?

Who isn't speaking?

What non-verbal messages are passing between members?

Are the lines of communication flowing, varied or rigid and

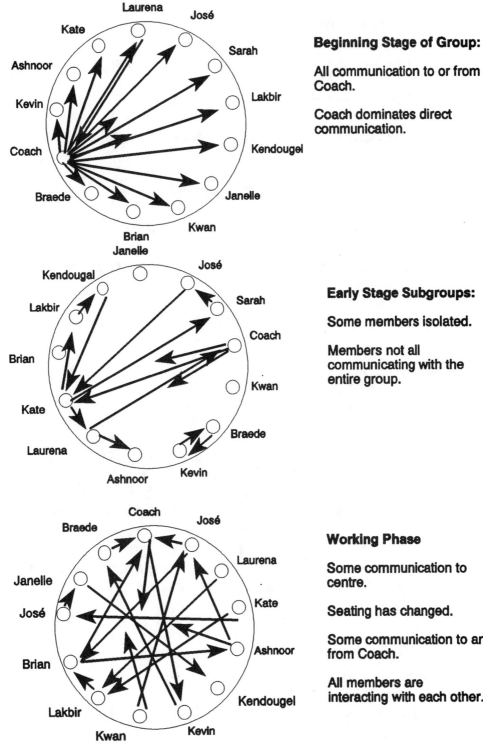

Beginning Stage of Group:

All communication to or from Coach.

Coach dominates direct communication.

Early Stage Subgroups:

Some members isolated.

Members not all communicating with the entire group.

Working Phase

Some communication to centre.

Seating has changed.

Some communication to and from Coach.

All members are interacting with each other.

Figure 15 Stages of Communication in Groups

stuck?

Why is the web lop-sided?

Who consistently supports, interrupts or disagrees with whom?

Who helps others enter the discussion?

How does the coach make an effort to relate to all participants equally?

What are the signs that feelings are not being expressed?

Whom do people look at when they talk?

Are leadership roles (task and maintenance) shared among members?

Or does everyone look to the coach to lead the group?

Physical Climate

Coaches need to be aware of the impact of the physical environment on the group. If air is stuffy or too cold (hot), chairs hard, room crowded or dull looking, learning can be impaired. Appropriate breaks assist participants' concentration. Local and external noises and poor lighting can irritate the group and affect how it functions. Flip charting needs to be large, interesting and easily read from the back of the room. A circle of chairs is considered the ideal set up for Life Skills groups. This arrangement facilitates discussion among all members of the group since everyone can be seen and heard.

Questions to Ask

Do participants need a break?

Are the participants able to sit on the floor, get up and move around when needed?

Do we need to open some windows, close doors?

Has the circle of chairs been maintained?

Are the flip charts clear, colourful and easily read?

Group Atmosphere: Emotional Climate, Trust and Safety

The emotional climate of a group can be open, warm and friendly or cool, formal, restrained or hostile. It will directly influence whether and how the members participate. The climate will encourage trust or mistrust among members. Individuals and groups can grow and flourish when there is trust. Trust is the essential ingredient in a group that makes it safe for members to learn in an open way with one another. Equally, members will remain closed if they do not feel safe.

Trusting behaviour is the willingness to risk consequences by making oneself vulnerable. Trustworthy behaviour is the willingness to be there for other people in a way that allows them to take risks.

All members are responsible for making the climate safe for one another in order to take risks. Explicit rules and guidelines developed and honoured by the group can help to build trust.

Questions to Ask

How is the atmosphere affecting the members' participation?

Do they feel included, safe or connected to the group?

Are the members risking self-disclosures?

Do they seem comfortable giving and receiving feedback?

In what ways are members taking risks?

Has the group developed its ground rules?

Are members honouring the confidentiality rule?

How can trust be developed in this group?

When would it be the right time to talk about trust, risk, self-disclosure in this group?

Group Cohesiveness

Cohesiveness relates to how attractive, safe and interesting the group is to its members. It reflects the morale and sense of team spirit. It is seen when members work together interdependently.

Questions to Ask

Are there any leadership (power) struggles?

Are participants free to be themselves (show their true colours)?

Who exhibits balanced self-determined (BSD) behaviour?

What are the signs that they are enjoying themselves and each other?

How are members taking care of each other while attending to the tasks?

Group Norms and Standards

Each group eventually develops acceptable topics and behaviour for working together. Norms are guidelines to help promote constructive interaction so that participants can feel safe and have an opportunity to contribute to group process.

Norms and standards can help stabilize the group. It is also important to note that groups can develop negative norms. Acceptable topics, behaviours and procedures can be normalized once the group has gone through its testing and stormy phase.

Questions to Ask

What are the norms that have developed in this group?

How openly do members discuss personal and group issues?

What topics have become "no-no's" for this group?

What are the norms regarding what can or can't be said or done?

Group Purpose and Goals

All groups need a goal(s) to function effectively. Groups can spend a great deal of their time determining their purpose or goals; others sum up their *raison d'être* and terms of reference in the first meeting. Until the purpose and goals are set, groups can flounder. Some goals are clear, specific and known to everyone; others are vague, implicit or hidden.

Goals can emerge from the group or be imposed. Ultimately, goals have to be agreed upon for a group to work effectively. A group will function more effectively and productively if it identifies its purpose both at the outset and whenever it gets bogged down.

Goals can either be determined by the coach, agency or program prior to members becoming a group. Or, goals can be negotiated and evolve during the life of the group. The latter is the ideal. Goals or needs are operating on two levels: espoused (declared) and practised, real (lived).

Declared or espoused goals:
Declared goals are those that have been articulated by the program or agreed upon by the group toward which the members may or may not be working. They have also been expressed in terms of *felt* needs in contrast with *real* needs. They are the outside reason people enrol in courses (for example, to become more marketable; to get a certificate; to learn how to...)

Real, practised or lived goals:
Real needs or goals are demonstrated in what members actually do in the group (voting with their feet). They underlie concerns

Verbal Participation

Who says a lot - little?
Attitudes toward them - how are they treated?
Patterns of interaction

Influence

Who has strong influence - little? Why?
Who do you naturally trust as a leader? Why?
Any leadership struggles?

Feedback and Risk-taking

Who gives really perceptive feedback?
Who only dares to give positive?
Who can give negative constructively?
Who risks in self-disclosure?
Who do you feel comfortable or uncomfortable with?

Maintenance

Who helps others get into the discussion?
Who really listens - clarifies for others?
Who are the peacemakers?
Who seems to see conflict as creative?

Membership

Sub-grouping?
Who consistently supports or disagrees with the same person?
Any outsiders? Insiders?

Feelings

Signs of feelings not expressed - tones, expressions, body postures, gestures?

Norms

What are the group norms regarding what can or can't be said or done?

Figure 16 Reading Group Dynamics

about inclusion (membership), control (conformity), need for clarity and personal relevance (purpose) and other hidden agendas. Real needs can be understood in terms of concerns such as:

- What am I going to get out of being in this group?

- Who will help me get my social, emotional or networking needs met?

- How much of my own needs am I willing to compromise here?

- What will this course get me?

- How much do I have to donate or sacrifice for success in this group?

Questions to Ask

What steps have been taken to ensure that participants understand the goals of the program?

Have they all 'bought into' what they are doing?

How explicit and inclusive was the agreement (contracting)?

Group Procedures and Decision-Making Methods

Every group develops specific ways of working together to get the tasks done. Procedures need to be adequate and appropriate to the task. It is helpful for groups to experience a variety of decision-making methods to know which ones are most appropriate for different problems encountered. Whether aware of it or not, groups are constantly making decisions (even when deciding <u>not</u> to do something).

Some decisions are consciously made related to the tasks at hand; others without awareness. It is important to observe and de-brief how decisions are made to assess appropriateness and whether members took on more than they realized (*We did decide to do "X" didn't we?*). Since silence is not always consent, methods such as consensus, designed to include all members of the group, need to be tried.

Consensus decision-making, though time consuming, may be best choice for an issue critically important to members. Consensus is not unanimity but agreement in principle by all. Consensus-testing is the genuine exploration to root out opposition and determine whether those who were in opposition can live comfortably with the decision.

Questions to Ask

Is interrupting permissible or does the group have a hands-up rule?

Does the group work with a written or verbal agenda?

Is it appropriate to have rotating or shared leadership?

When are consensus seeking methods used? when not?

How does the group ensure that everyone has a voice in decision-making?

Does the group pretend to listen to everyone but do what the most vocal members want in the end?

Stages of Group Development

Leadership is any behaviour which influences the group's direction and way of working together. The degree of control needed to lead a group depends on the existing balance of task, maintenance and self-oriented behaviour within the group.

At the outset, the coach initiates and models leadership behaviour in both task and maintenance areas. Once the group is established, the coach encourages members to share the leadership roles with him/her.

Research on group dynamics has identified several, predictable stages through which all groups typically move. One model developed by Zenger (Figure 17)[3] is particularly effective in that it describes the phases of the group in terms of stages of human development.

One of the best known models of group development is the one articulated by Bruce Tuckman[4]. To identify the stages, Tuckman used the terms *forming, storming, norming* and *performing*.

Added to his model is the final stage, leaving or *adjourning*, indicating a typical process which groups experience as they begin to separate.

Other, more playful terms that have been used to describe these stages are:

- groping
- griping
- grasping
- grouping

Groping characterizes the first stage where members are confused about their roles and what the group is all about. Griping is a period when members are in conflict and concerned about losing or keeping control. Grasping is when they are making an effort to move beyond self-serving interests and grasping the concept of working as a group. Grouping happens once the group has found a way to work together effectively.

Using the more well known Tuckman model, the following discussion outlines some of the processes typifying each stage.

Stage One: Forming

During this stage, members are dependent on the leader. This stage is analogous to the infant in human development. Members have not yet bought the idea that this is *their* group. There can be

---

[3]John H. Zenger, *A Comparison of Human Development with Psychological Development in Training Groups*, Training and Development, July 1970.

[4]Bruce Tuckman, Development Sequence in Small Groups, in *Psychological Bulletin*, 1965, 63 (6).

Stages of Development	Intellectual Dimension	Emotional Dimension	Communication Model	Interaction of Intellectual and Emotional Dimension	Representative Behaviour
Infant	What is this? Little cognitive understanding	Safety, security, self-concept preservation. Response to own viscera. Response to emotions from others.	Receiving communication. Output is only social noise.	Conflicting.	Dependency.
Child	Make sense of environment, order it, develop some beginning understanding.	Extension of safety and security needs.	Some response to communication from others. Minimum of listening.	Partially supporting.	Attempts to organize. Exploring. Function an individuals.
Adolescent	What can I get out of this?	Need for acceptance and belonging. Expression of peaks and valleys of emotion.	Understands communication but often disagrees.	Conflicting.	Rejection of authority. Dependency and counter-dependency. Blaming.
Young Adult	What can I learn from this? It is possible to learn from peers. Understand goals and objectives of training.	Awareness of own feelings and emotions of others. Acceptance of inadequacies. Recognition for what I really am.	Sharing.	Basically congruent.	Sharing information. Levelling. Openness.
Adult	Desire to find out more about self and others. Discuss emotions from intellectual viewpoint. What can I give to this?	High value on authenticity. Acceptance of others, concern for feelings, desires for warmth, closeness. Desire for growth.	Sharing as equals.	Congruent.	Self-direction. Wider participation. Useful structure. Leadership shared. Both negative and positive expressions are acceptable.

Figure 17 Summary of Stages of Group Development

both excitement and anxiety about the unknown. Members begin tentatively to explore what behaviour is acceptable for this group and how they will fit in.

Major Focus

- concern about inclusion, belonging, acceptance, rejection

- difference is emphasized over similarities at this stage

- concern about course requirements, expectations

- want to be oriented and introduced to the tasks

- suspicious, anxious about what this group is all about

Typical Behaviour

- polite, cautious small talk

- concern about impression (best foot forward)

- dependence on the leader

- hesitant participation

- intellectual or evasive

Unconscious and Conscious Thoughts

Who are these people? (They are/have: more/less education; younger/older, different orientation/abilities/ethnicities than I...).

What is expected of me? What are the roles and rules?

What will this course/task be like?

What are the goals? What are we expected to do?

Can I commit to this project?

Stage Two: Storming

Once people get to know one another and have their questions dealt with through an orientation process (goals and expectations outlined), the group moves on to the next stage, namely, storming. Some may feel that the group is not "real" and provocative behaviour may begin to stir things up. Issues of control begin to surface. Members become hostile or overzealous as a way to exercise control; they are demonstrating their resistance to losing their individuality and becoming a "group".

Thus, storming happens when resistance builds in the group. There can be resistance toward a member, the leader and the group in general. The group lacks unity; cliques and alliances may form and conflict is often evident. In terms of human development, this stage is analogous to adolescence during which minimal positive emotions are expressed; pessimism and restlessness can dominate.

<u>Major Focus</u>

- concerned about status, power, control, authority, conflict

- move into more risky, controversial topics and ways of working together

- authority figure issues from the past surface

- resist doing tasks which are seen as overshadowing personal needs

- polarization of group members

- concern about pecking order

<u>Typical Behaviour</u>

- power struggles

- criticism of leader

- conflict among members

- self-righteous and judgemental

- quieter members discuss issues at breaks rather than in group

- riskier self-disclosure and feedback among members

<u>Unconscious and Conscious Thoughts</u>

I want input; I need to be heard.

How am I being judged? Evaluated?

I need to let so-and-so know how I am really feeling about this.

Who decides what we should be doing?

What are the rules?

What's the point of all this?

I haven't got time for this garbage!

We never did that in my other group!

Stage Three: Norming

During this stage, the group experiences a breakthrough in their process. An event often catalyses the previous collection of self-serving individuals into a collective. One member may speak up and honestly reveal his or her true feelings of insecurity and/or positive regard for other members.

The coach whose influence had waned, is now seen as stronger than before. Allowing a group to find its own way through the storm rather than control the process takes courage on the part of the coach. In terms of human development, this group process represents growing into young adulthood.

Once participants feel that they have taken risks airing their concerns, the group has moved into the norming stage. Since they now feel they have a voice and are being taken seriously, they can shift the focus from self to group. Members begin to accept the idea of working as a team and the quirks of other members of the group. Norms such as implicit and explicit rules or guidelines that the group has agreed to follow are being developed and solidified at this stage to help them work as a collective.

Major Focus

• group building and maintenance roles more polished

• need to work interdependently

• different leadership roles shared by many members

• concern about rules organization, agenda order, agreement

• tolerance of differences

• efforts to achieve harmony

• new sense of team

• members find their place in the group

• more comfortable making mistakes

Typical Behaviour

• willing to try new behaviour, take risks

• listening, openness, genuine sharing

• silent members feel safer to speak up directly

• win/win approach

• sharing ideas rather than grandstanding

• willing to change for the sake of the group

<u>Conscious and Unconscious Thoughts</u>

I do not need to show off my brilliance if something has already been said.

I am going to agree to disagree rather than prolong the discussion.

I am starting to look forward to coming to this group.

Stage Four: Performing

Once the group feels that they have established ground rules for how to work together, it moves on to the next stage, namely, performing. It becomes an entity capable of solving problems, resolving differences and making decisions effectively. In terms of human development, the parallel stage is adulthood. This stage is characterized by self-determination, caring for others and productivity. The mature individual can receive criticism without being destroyed and accepts warmth and affection without being unduly embarrassed.

<u>Major Focus</u>

• high commitment, warmth

• members care for one another

• cohesion and commitment to task and group

• members would rather function effectively than be "right"

<u>Typical Behaviour</u>

• effective problem-solving

• healthy joking, affection and playfulness

• supportive and encouraging one another

• accepting and valuing differences

- leadership roles continue to be shared

<u>Conscious and Unconscious Thoughts</u>

How can I help things run more smoothly?

I feel good about working as a team.

I like what I am learning.

I am proud of the way we are working together!

Stage Five: Adjourning

Groups about to disband often go through *separation anxiety*. If the group has been a positive experience, this can be a time of strong feelings. The "letting go" and grieving process is not unlike that felt over other losses in life. In fact, unfinished business from past losses may re-surface at this time for some individuals.

At this point, groups appreciate the leader taking charge and helping them through the final stage. Typically, they like to evaluate their learning and the course, acknowledge one another, receive feedback on their positive contributions to the group and share recollections about the time spent together.

In human development terms, this stage is parallel to older **adults** wanting to review the highlights and revel in accomplishments of their life.

<u>Major Focus</u>

- concern about disengaging from one another

- evaluate group and personal accomplishments

- grieving

- keen to apply new learning

- getting ready to leave

- preparing for next step

- sorting out old wounds and losses

- some fear of the future

<u>Typical Behaviour</u>

- confused about feelings

- dependence on the leader returns

- lethargy

- grief: acting out, fight or flight responses, sadness

- discuss ways to apply the learning to outside situation

- ultimately accepts that the reason for the group no longer exists and it is time to move on

<u>Conscious and Unconscious Thoughts</u>

I am ready to move on.

I will miss this group.

I don't know what I will do with my time once this group ends.

I am both excited and afraid about the next step.

Who needs this group?

I don't think I can face coming to the last class.

Finally, it is important to remember "the map is not the territory". The map or model of group development is meant simply as a guide for groups and coaches to use when looking at their own processes.

While groups go through stages identified in the research on groups, it is important to point out that individual growth does not necessarily overlap with the group stages. Obviously, participants will not learn exactly the same thing from the experience. Yet on some level, everyone is affected by having been part of the group.

> The true significance of the group experience may be that it provides a complete cycle through human psychological growth, leading to higher levels of maturity. Individuals whose own growth has been stopped at infant or child levels get the <u>exercise</u> of moving toward emotional adulthood. They see others sprint far beyond them...witnessing others progress to higher plateaus provides a model to strive for and a certainty that higher emotional plateaus exist...emotional stretching is good for our personalities. Like hikers going up a mountain, some are in the lead and others trail. Many may never reach the top. Yet, in the process, everyone is pulled to a higher level than where they started.[5]

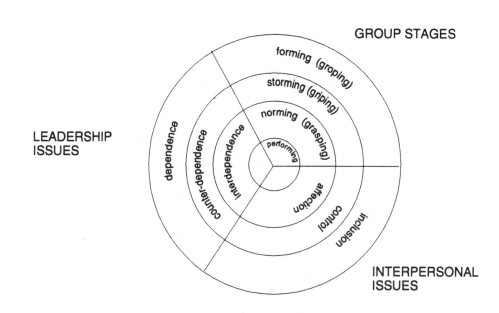

Figure 18 Leadership and Stages of Group

---

[5]Ibid., p. 86.

5.3 Behaviour and Communication in Groups

Defense Mechanisms in Groups

Not all groups sail through the developmental stages. Some groups stay locked in an earlier stage such as the forming, polite or storming, testy ones. Discussing the stages and looking at its own process, can help a group move into the performing stage.

At times, participants find that learning about themselves, trying out unfamiliar behaviour and finding out how their behaviour affects others, can be very unnerving. In unit four, the concept of "conscious incompetence" was explored. This phase in learning a new behaviour is characterized as frustrating and awkward. It is the point when learners are feeling acutely aware that they have not yet integrated a new behaviour. Resistance is a common response to learning in groups because it can be frightening and demanding.

The group tends to put subtle and sometimes not-so-subtle, pressures on individuals to self-disclose, take risks, confront, share their feelings honestly. These pressures can produce feelings of inadequacy, anxiety, shame, guilt and other disturbing emotions.

It is natural that learners will try to avoid such feelings and pressures. Avoidance behaviour is a defense mechanism which tends to be unconscious.

Another way of thinking about defense mechanisms is in terms of the flight-fight response to stress. In the flight response, a person retreats from the situation. In the fight response, a person attacks or engages others. A third response is called "pairing" in which an individual manipulates and lobbies for support in the belief that there is safety in numbers.

The following section discusses behaviour out of context. In other words, it is important to view defensive behaviour in the context of the group dynamics and stages of development. It may be that individuals are taking care of themselves in unsafe conditions or resisting change. However, if participants consistently hide behind defense mechanisms, others in the group will likely give them feedback about the effect of their behaviour on them. These individuals can choose to modify their behaviour to fall in with the group norm. This decision can affect whether the group will function in a performing way.

An important role for the facilitator is to try to make the group as safe as possible by helping the group set ground rules and allow participants to enter the group when ready. However, another role for the leader might be to help the participants see their defensive responses by giving feedback. A sensitive coach will know when and how to intervene.

Examples of Defense Mechanisms

Flight

<u>Withdrawing</u>

- demonstrates boredom

- shows non-verbally that they have tuned out

- deals with other issues to avoid the issue at hand

<u>Intellectualizing</u>

- psychologizes, therapizes others to take focus off self

- deals with emotions objectively

- dazzles with language skills

<u>Generalizing</u>

- makes sweeping statements about how "they", "you", "one" feels about certain things to avoid saying what they themselves are feeling

Fight

Projecting

- attributes characteristics to another that are unacceptable to themselves

Interrogating

- cross-examines others to keep the spotlight off themselves

Competing

- argues with everyone including the leader to avoid dealing with own issues

Blaming

- constantly complains that nothing is working; makes others feel inadequate and keeps the focus off themselves

Pairing

Sub-grouping
- colludes and forms sub-groups with others for emotional support to avoid dealing with issues

Scapegoating
- undue attention is spent on one individual who does not fit the norm, keeping the action away from others of the group

Dealing with the above behaviour is not an easy task for even the most seasoned group member or coach. As a coach, one of the best interventions is to design and present a lesson dealing with observable issues and behaviour. For example, a lesson on helpful and hindering group behaviour or on stress responses (fight-flight), could provide members with an understanding of their actions without being confronted directly.

If avoidance behaviour still persists, the coach could decide that the next approach would be one-on-one sensitive, genuine "I" messages, modelling rules for effective feedback.

Helpful and Hindering Group Behaviours

Members of a group have two kinds of needs: the need to accomplish a task and the need to work effectively as a group. Behaviour can be classified in terms of task and maintenance functions. Task roles include behaviour required to carry out a group task; maintenance or group building roles include behaviour required to strengthens and maintain group life and activities. Most behaviour contains elements of both task and maintenance roles.

Behaviour which meets group needs, strengthens group interaction and helps in the development of problem-solving skills is considered to be helpful.

The coach and group members need to understand the dynamics of both helpful and hindering behaviour in order to accomplish individual and group goals. Generally, hindering behaviour should be promptly pointed out and dealt with by the affected member of the group.

The following are examples of hindering and helpful group behaviour.

Hindering Group Behaviour

Hindering behaviour can affect group members progress in problem-solving and personal development. It tends to make the group as a whole inefficient or weak.

Being Aggressive

- tries to improve status by criticizing or blaming others

- shows hostility towards group or an individual

- deflates the status of others

What to Do

- feedback is the best intervention to deal with the person who is hostile

- be aware of intentions (to help or to hurt?)

- do not dump; rather, inform in a face-saving way

  I sense you're feeling angry/impatient...

Blocking

- interferes with progress of the group by going off on a tangent

- cites personal experiences unrelated to the group problem or purpose

- rejects ideas without consideration

- argues too long on a point

What to Do

- When the blocker pauses for breath, take this opportunity to intervene.

  I'd like to get back to the subject of...

Competing

- vies with others to produce the best idea

- talks the most

- plays the most roles

- tries to gain favour with the group leader

- vies with leader for power

What to Do

- open it up and/or contribute:

  I'd like to hear some of the other ideas.

  I have a need to share my idea also..

Seeking Sympathy

- tries to attract sympathy for personal problems or misfortunes

- disparages own ideas to gain support

- plays victim

- whines about their life or the group

What to Do

- to move the member to consider solutions, try the following:

  If we come up with a reasonable solution, will you try it?

Special Pleading

- introduces or supports ideas related to pet concerns or philosophies

- lobbies others for support

- attempts to use the group as an audience regarding unrelated matters

What to Do

- stick to the subject of the discussion

- refocus group by pointing out that the discussion has wandered

I would like to get back to ...

Horsing Around

- clowns, jokes around

- occasional humour is welcome and is often helpful for relieving tension; however, relentless horsing around needs to be challenged

What to Do

- identify flight mode in group

  What is going on here? Can we get back to business now?

Seeking Recognition

- calls attention to self by loud or excessive talking, extreme ideas or unusual behaviour

What to Do

- if someone is playing the one-up game, offer some feedback:

  Thanks for your ideas! I'm concerned that others haven't had input...

Withdrawing

- acts indifferently or passively

- resorts to icy formality

- daydreams

- doodles

- whispers to others

- wanders from the subject

What to Do

- Try to include withdrawn person into the discussion.

  I'd like to hear from you. We need a fresh approach...

Foreclosing

- assumes the problem is solved before consensus has been reached

- tries to cut of decision prematurely

What to Do

- Check if the group is ready to end the process by asking:

  Have we reached agreement on this or do we need to discuss it further?

- Listen carefully if other members' contributions come from a different understanding of the problem and find out what they are talking about.

Minimizing

- assuming the problem is not important

What to Do

- If the problem seems unimportant to you, ask to find out what meaning it has for others. The response will either reveal that others want to move to another issue or that there is valid the reason it is important to the group.

  How serious is this problem?

Helpful Group Behaviour

Task Behaviours

Initiating

- proposes solutions and new ideas

- suggests a new definition of the problem or way of organizing information

  My sense is we have a new problem we haven't yet considered...

Seeking Information

- asks for clarification of suggestions or ideas

- requests additional facts or information

  Are there any articles available on this subject?

  Would you elaborate on what services the ABC agency has to offer?

Seeking Opinion

- solicits ideas from the members

- seeks clarification of values, suggestions or ideas

  What do you think our bottom line should be?

  Should this be one of our possible solutions?

Giving Information

- offers relevant facts or ideas

- relates own experience to the group problem to illustrate points

There was something in the paper about that last week. It said...

When I had a similar problem I tried that and ...

Giving Opinion

- states opinion or belief concerning a suggestion or an idea, particularly concerning its value rather than its factual basis

I think it would be better to wait until I can pay cash.

I might accomplish more if I were given more positive feedback...

Elaborating

- clarifies meaning

- gives examples

- envisions how a proposal might work if adopted

If we tackled this problem now, it would have the further advantage of ...

Are you saying that if Luis were to force his son to apologize, this might make the boy all the more resentful?

Coordinating

- shows relationships between ideas or suggestions

- pulls ideas together

- draws together the activities of various subgroups or members

Perhaps your suggestion for getting Maria's co-operation would be just as valuable as Juan's idea, because both suggestions involve ...

Summarizing

- restates suggestions from the group members

Where are we now? Kaelin has proposed we wait until we are all here; Horace suggested we develop a plan for the others to react to...

Maintenance Behaviours

Encouraging

- supports by being friendly, warm, responsive to others

- praises others and their ideas

- acknowledges and accepts contributions from others

You were talking about that last week. Maybe your experience would help us at this point.

That's a great idea! How did it work when you tried it out?

You seem doubtful about this idea, Paul. I'd like to hear what you think about it.

Gatekeeping

- makes it possible for another member to make a contribution to the group by asking that person to speak

- suggests limited talking time for everyone so that all will have a chance to be heard

You look like you have something to say on this.

Just a minute, I think some of the others would like to comment on this point.

I'd like to hear some other views on this. Is there anyone else who hasn't spoken who would like to?

I'd like to hear Wyn finish developing her idea. (When she has been interrupted.)

Standard Setting

- expresses or reviews standards for the group to use in choosing its content or procedures

- reminds the group to avoid decisions which conflict with its standards

Let's decide if this topic (or approach) is appropriate for our group?

Have we a need to address the issue of late arrivals?

Expressing Group Feeling

- summarizes the group feeling

- describes group's reaction to ideas or solutions

It seems that everyone agreed to list this as one of our possible solutions.

My sense is we're disturbed at the thought of...

I hear people saying they have no objection on moral grounds, but that it wouldn't make a very effective solution.

I sense more hesitation in the group. We're agreeing, but we don't sound very certain about it.

Relieving Tension

- drains off negative feeling by jesting

- puts a tense situation in wider context

At this stage, we don't have to agree with each other, do we? We're still in the discussion stage. Let's hear what someone else has to say!

I think we're all getting tired - let's take a coffee break now.

Task and Maintenance Roles Combined

Diagnosing

- determines source of difficulty and appropriate steps to take

- analyzes main blocks to progress

  We seem to be rushed to get a decision before lunch. Can we agree to resume our discussion later if necessary?

  I've noticed that every time Maria makes a suggestion, it gets attacked.

Testing for Consensus

- asks for group opinion to determine whether the group is nearing consensus on a decision

- sends up "trial balloons" to test group opinions

  Are we ready to accept solution C?

  Are we ready to leave this now and go on to the next idea?

Mediating and Harmonizing

- conciliates different points of view

- offers compromise solutions

  If this plan is not fully acceptable to everyone, how about changing it to ...?

  It seems that you both want to see the misunderstanding cleared up - the only disagreement is on how to do it. Maybe we can think of ways that will be acceptable to everyone.

6

Coaching and Facilitation Skills

A good facilitator is a guide on the side, not a sage on the stage

6.1   Life Skills Coaching Defined

Life Skills Coaching and Facilitating

As facilitators, the tasks of the Life Skills coach are to facilitate problem-solving, create a safe climate and manage conflict. These goals are accomplished by helping groups identify their purpose, goals, issues and resources both within and outside the group.

As well, coaches model and teach helpful group behaviours, share their own experiences, resources and processes in the service of the group goals. It is also their role to help group members accomplish their goals and to encourage the group to look at its development and ways of working together.

In the previous unit, various aspects of group dynamics were explored so that coaches would have a language and conceptual framework to help them facilitate processes within their groups. It was assumed that all groups have similar basic characteristics at different stages of their development. Members also demonstrate typical behaviour in dealing with issues facing groups. These can be summarized in four categories: membership, communication, goal clarity and control or leadership issues.

In this unit, some of the dynamics discussed previously are addressed from the point of view of the leader, with implications for intervention decisions and styles. First, there is a general discussion on leadership styles, then an overview of what characterizes a facilitator and finally, a look at coaching issues. The assumption is that a coach is a leader who acts as a facilitator, trainer and co-learner in Life Skills groups.

Difference Between A Facilitator And Coach

A coach is a facilitator, but a facilitator is not necessarily a coach.

A facilitator in the purest sense, is an objective outsider to the group process whose job is to help manage the process. Coaches, on the other hand, have a more vested interest and become more personally involved as role models. Coaches are "participants with expertise".

While they are not objective observers, coaches also need to know when to take an unbiased position; for example, when the group is in conflict or when values are being discussed if the coach is not directly affected or implicated.

Knowing when to self-disclose and be part of the group as a co-learner and when to step back while others work out their differences can be a challenge. There is a fine line between the two positions. Ideally, all coaches need supervision whether in the form of a mentor or support group to help work out their own value struggles and issues lest they use the group for their own ends.

While facilitators, again in the purest sense, help groups to stick to the agenda or task, coaches recognize that important learning can happen as a result of going off-track to meet group needs and dealing with "here and now" issues.

The concept, "the process is the content" discussed earlier, applies here. If groups need to abandon the task in order to work on their process (how they are functioning as a group), then that becomes the learning for that moment. To teach problem-solving, (conflict resolution, stress management, BSD behaviour) and not deal with these issues as they occur in the group, would be inconsistent with the Life Skills philosophy.

While teachers and trainers teach and facilitators are experts in group process, coaches have expertise in both content and process. They need to be flexible and know when and how to move back and forth between the two.

6.2 Group Leadership

What is a Leader?

Intervention Styles

Before outlining different leadership styles, it is important to clarify that leadership behaviour is not confined to facilitators or coaches. Ideally, all group members perform leadership functions when they are ready.

It is also important to point out that *influence* and *participation* are not the same dynamic. *Influence* can be positive or negative; it can rally or alienate the group. Members' responses to someone who is trying to influence them can be either *open* or *closed*.

Some members are high participators who talk a lot. This does not mean they are necessarily influential, in the sense that others are really listening to them. On the other hand, others are low participators who rarely speak; yet, when they do, they command the attention of the whole group. So too, with facilitator styles. Some leaders may have a high profile; others low. Added to this, coaches, each with different temperaments and learning styles will influence groups in different ways.

The following outline of different influencing styles relates to both coaches and participants. Four basic styles have been identified in the literature studying leadership behaviour.

Directive

- attempts to impose their perspective or values onto others

- tries to win support through coercion, bullying, blocking other ideas or approaches if they do not fit their own

- rallies the group to move when a decision needs to be made quickly

- has high control needs

Harmonizer

- agrees with everyone for the sake of peace

- pours oil on troubled waters

- has high inclusion, belonging needs

- avoids dealing with negative feelings and conflict

Laissez Faire

- does not take a stand one way or the other

- seems not to care about what is going on or the results

- believes that others can work things out among themselves

- is easy-going

- trusts the process

Democratic

- makes an effort to include everyone in discussions

- expresses own feelings and opinions openly and directly

- mediates without taking sides

- considers what the fair way would be for all parties

Flexible

- is conversant with all styles and can be flexible

- shifts style according to the needs and abilities of the group at different stages of its development

- is able to assess the maturity level of the group

- knows when to be directive, laissez-faire or democratic

Situational Leadership Model

In late seventies, Paul Hersey and Ken Blanchard developed the Situational Leadership Model[1] in which they challenged the idea that there was a "best" style of leadership. They claim that successful leaders are those who can adapt their behaviour to meet the needs of the situation or group. The terms they use for different styles at different stages are: telling (directive), selling (persuading), participating (collaborating) and delegating (monitoring).

The situational model allows for all styles of leadership to be used depending on the stage or maturity level of the group. "Maturity" refers to the capacity to set attainable goals and the willingness and ability to take responsibility for carrying these out. As the group grows in its sophistication to handle both the task (goals) and ways of working together (relationship or maintenance behaviour), leaders shift their style accordingly.
Task behaviour is the extent to which a leader explains what (when, where, how) the group is to do something, while relationships behaviour is providing emotional support while working on the task.

A situational theory of behaviour is based on the amount of direction (task-oriented) and the amount of emotional support

---

[1]Paul Hersey and Ken Blanchard, *Situational Leadership*, (reprint) University Associates, 1976.

(relationship-oriented) a leader must provide relative to the situation and maturity or "readiness" level of the group.
The assumption is that groups start at low levels of maturity and with appropriate interventions and flexibility from the leader, will develop to a point where they become self-managing. Under ideal conditions, the leaders have done themselves out of a job and indigenous leaders are trained.

Figure 19 looks at leadership styles and stages of group development. It can be a helpful framework for considering an appropriate and responsible intervention.

6.3   Roles of the Life Skills Coach

Facilitation

A true facilitator is one who guides problem-solving, manages conflicts and helps the group maintain a positive, safe climate for learning or working together. The facilitator's main concern is dealing with process issues. There are two parts to this process: helping to keep the group focused (task) and maintaining the ground rules for working together (relationship or maintenance).

Facilitators keep the group moving, help the members stay focused on the agreed upon task, encourage reflection and remain "group" as opposed to "self" oriented.

In helping to maintain the group, facilitators assist group members to honour rules or norms that have been established. For example, they do not allow people to be cornered or bullied; they find ways to give everyone a chance to participate; they diffuse loaded language; they help to direct monopolizers and encourage quiet ones to speak up more. In this latter role, they are also known as "conversational traffic cops".

Facilitator's Responsibilities

• observes group process

Stage	Group	Leadership Style
Forming (infant)	Dependent Inclusion needs high	Telling Directing Guiding Low Relationship High Task
Storming (adolescence)	Counter-dependent Control needs high	Selling Persuading Clarifying High Relationship High Task
Norming (young adult)	Affection needs high	Participating Encouraging Collaborating Committing High Relationship Low Task
Performing (mature adult)	Interdependent Needs are met Confident	Delegating Observing Monitoring Low Relationship Low Task
Adjourning (retirement)	Independent, dependent and interdependent	Directing Bringing Closure High Relationship High Task

Figure 19 Leadership Styles and Stages of Group Development

- helps keep group focused

- discourages groups from going off-topic

- ensures that everyone participates

- protects members from getting attacked

- points out and helps to resolve conflicts

As mentioned, a Life Skills coach is a facilitator, but the reverse is not necessarily true. The above outline of a facilitator describes only one of the many hats that a coach wears.

A coach's primary tool is the Life Skills lesson. The lesson is the first intervention used in helping groups identify helpful and hindering behaviour in groups. In this role, the coach is a trainer or even teacher. However, once the ideas and skills are put into practice, Life Skills leaders become facilitators, co-learners (as role modellers), behavioural counsellors or human relations coaches. Given the potential for confusion about the role of the coach, leaders should clearly define their roles and responsibilities and demonstrate that their style will shift depending on the needs and stages of the group.

Modelling

Life Skills coaching is one type of helping activity. A coach is a special kind of helper, an agent of change. In addition to designing and delivering Life Skills lessons, another key role for the coach is to demonstrate authenticity.

From earliest childhood, a great deal of learning which takes place is imitative. Commonly, children imitate the behaviour of significant people in their lives. Imitative learning continues in adulthood. As a Life Skills coach who has integrated many of the skills, modelling behaviour for others is a very powerful intervention. The behaviour modelled by other group members can be likewise be a strong influence for imitative learning.

Learning about self and others is a life-long process for both students and coaches alike. Techniques and lesson ideas can be read in manuals and texts, but the reality is that the coach's presentation of self is a significant factor in learning. For this reason, Life Skills Coaches Training courses and workshops are designed to help coaches continue this process of personal growth and learning.

The Helping Process

Helping then, is a transforming process. The effectiveness of the helping process is determined by the relationship which develops between the coach and the student. There are two behavioural components to helping in this sense; namely, responsive and initiative behaviour.

The responsive component is made up of attending behaviours used in conjunction with empathy, respect and attention to specifics. The initiative component is made up of attending behaviours used in conjunction with genuineness, confrontation and attention to timing.

As the coach models these dynamics, students learn to be honest and authentic, to challenge their own excuses and face problems as they arise. As the coach both says and does ("walks the walk"), the students become more conscious of their behaviours in the moment, rather than in retrospect. They go through a process of self-exploration in specific and immediate situations. Self-evaluation leads to insight and understanding.

With self-awareness and with the example of the coach's and members' behaviours in their mind, the students can become motivated to act. At this point, if it is starting to mean something to them, it is not uncommon for the students to "buy into" the Life Skills group process. In turn, the students will be able to use the same dynamics in their interactions with others. Practice, use, teach (PUT) is a key Life Skills motto.

In a helping relationship where the coach is communicating responsive and initiative components at appropriate levels, the students become aware that their own communications are being understood, validated and reflected back to them with sensitivity and accuracy. This results in students really listening to themselves. They may begin to engage in introspection of themselves, their belief systems and assumptions about the world.

Through this process, they may be moved to re-examine their understanding of themselves. In order for this development to occur, the coach's communications must show a balance between warmth and sensitivity on the one hand, backbone and challenge on the other. Many students progress toward self-direction and self-control once they have experienced constructive and helpful feedback and reinforcement.

Self-exploration leads to self-understanding. Understanding is manifested in action which in turn results in feedback and reinforcement which leads to further exploration and so on. The learning cycle becomes a continuous process of self-improvement.

Rescuing

Rescuing is to be distinguished from helping others to help themselves. This concept is captured in the oft-quoted saying which notes that there is a huge difference between feeding a person a fish for a day and teaching that person how to fish for a lifetime. This is one way to distinguish between rescuing and helping. The first position sends the meta-message that people cannot take care of themselves and need to be rescued. The second position holds that people can learn and are capable of taking care of themselves.

While rescuers may have good intentions at the conscious level, their interference can be very disempowering and damaging to the other person's self-esteem. They may well be avoiding looking at their own issues and feelings by focusing on someone else in the name of helping.

The same premise underlies the Life Skills model which focuses on teaching, modelling, facilitating and coaching rather than doing for others what they can do for themselves.

What to do:

Phase I in the Helping Process

Three ways to be responsive in phase I of working with students:

Empathy: coach tries to understand how the students experience the world by trying to see things through their eyes

Respect: coach communicates his or her belief that the students have the potential to manage their lives effectively and that it matters that they do so

Specificity: coach helps the students be very specific about feelings, experiences and perceptions of self and their world

Phase II in the Helping Process

Three ways to initiate in phase II of working with students:

Genuineness: coach tries to represent him or herself as authentically as possible

Confrontation: coach uses this dynamic in pointing out blind spots and inconsistencies between their declared self-perception and their actions

Immediacy: coach focuses on the "here and now" events in the relationship

Phase III in the Helping Process

Coaching: coach is most helpful in the third phase by assisting students to plan, implement and evaluate action for dealing with problems

Facilitating: coach encourages the group to support and share resources with one another

Figure 20 The Helping Process

Supervision

As has been discussed, Life Skills coaches have many roles and varied responsibilities. Coaches may face demands from students, agencies and funders. They may encounter situations in group that they had not anticipated. There can be a great deal of stress related to Life Skills coaching. Although coaches may share reactions and feelings in their Life Skills groups, it is never appropriate for coaches to do their own personal problem-solving there.

Having qualified coach training is not sufficient. It is essential that coaches receive support, feedback and guidance on an ongoing basis. This can best be accomplished through regular supervision with a manager, other Life Skills coaches or with a mentor.

In these sessions, coaches have an opportunity to vent feelings, share concerns and gain resources and insights. They have a chance to examine their personal coaching styles, values and find new approaches to deal with difficulties encountered in their Life Skills groups.

Additionally, coaches need to engage in professional development activities: workshops, seminars or refresher courses to enhance their learning and general sense of well being.

Coaches must continue to grow and learn beyond the coach training period. Supervision is an integral part of the Life Skills coaching process.

Advocacy

More and more, advocacy is becoming a central role for the Life Skills coach. The Houghton-Mifflin Canadian Dictionary defines advocate as: "to speak in favour of; recommend; a person who argues for a cause; supporter or defender"; and advocacy as: "active support, as of a cause."

Coaches may need to advocate for the rights of an individual, the group as a whole and/or the program. It is vital for people who have some power to use their own (or organization's) influence to gain access to resources unavailable to those most disenfranchised in society. Coaches must expand their roles beyond that of a group facilitator. Advocacy takes place on many different levels: the sponsoring organization, outside agencies (educational, health and social services), funders, government bureaucracies, local and global communities.

7

The Life Skills Program

7.1 Program Planning

Building a Life Skills Program

There is no one plan for mounting a Life Skills program. Many factors are at play in programming. However, despite varied factors, the course can remain true to the tenets and philosophy of the methodology.

Determining Purpose

The main determining factor is the mandate for the Life Skills program. This mandate and thus the objectives may be set by the funders of the organization. It may be set by the agency itself or by the community. However, the Life Skills coach needs to advocate for the type of program that will allow for maximum learning and empowerment of learners through Life Skills.

In settings which follow the Life Skills philosophy and methodology, coaches, in consultation with the organization and the community (often through an advisory committee), ideally have the flexibility to set up the program to meet the needs of the participants. Sometimes, a coach is asked to present a program that has been developed by the agency, with little option for flexibility. These programs may contain elements of the Life Skills model, but are not truly Life Skills programs.

Life Skills programs are offered in a wide variety of settings. Some examples are:

- career and employment training programs
- mental health settings
- correctional institutions
- women's groups
- men's groups
- high schools
- immigrant groups
- businesses
- spiritual organizations
- community colleges

Several factors might be considered in designing and setting up a Life Skills program.

Intake Criteria

Although one of the main principles of Life Skills is that coaches accept individuals at their present functioning level of behaviour, this does not preclude establishing criteria for intake. These criteria might be mandated by the organization or suggested by the community.

Based on the mandate of the funder, the limitations of the agency or the value of working exclusively with specific groupings, some possible criteria might be:

- gender
- literacy
- residence in the agency/institution
- homogeneity/heterogeneity
- age
- disability
- previous contact with the mental health/correction system
- current substance abuse
- ethnicity
- language
- prerequisite for further skill training

Physical Location

The physical climate of the Life Skills program is essential to developing and maintaining a positive and safe learning environment. The physical environment includes:

- locale of the program
- proximity to public transportation
- privacy of the room
- lighting
- windows
- furniture (moveable)
- wheel chair accessibility
- space for child care (if required)
- decor (colour, floor, wall and window covering)
- availability of washrooms, telephone
- beverages or refreshments if required
- space for small group activity
- individual space
- temperature control

Number and Length of Sessions

The number of sessions that constitute a Life Skills program will often be determined by the mandate of the organization. For instance, some agencies will offer Life Skills training as infrequently as once a week for ten weeks. Other agencies offer Life Skills groups five days a week for four to six months. The longer the program, the more Life Skills sessions, the better the integration of problem-solving behaviour.

Likewise, there is no prescribed length for a Life Skills session. Much will depend upon the composition of the group. However, if the coach is to proceed with all the phases of the lesson, two hours would appear to be the minimum length of time for a session. Appropriate breaks assist participants' concentration.

Group Size

Once again, it is often economics and/or funder's mandate that will determine group size. Ideally, the Life Skills group consists of ten to twelve members and no more than fifteen.

Program Design

Curriculum/Content of Lessons

The curriculum for a Life Skills course is determined by the objectives of the program, the number and length of sessions, combined with the predicted needs of the participants.

Lessons come from all of the five areas of Life Skills - self, family, community, job and leisure.

If the Life Skills group is part of a pre-employment training program, the emphasis is naturally on the area of employment or training. Other programs might have a different focus. However, lessons from all five areas are to be presented to facilitate the transferability of generic skills and behaviour.

Structure of Lessons

Once the rationale has been decided and the goals stated, the format of lessons follows the phases identified earlier in Unit 3.

- Stimulus
- Evocation
- Objective Enquiry
- Skills Practise
- Application
- Evaluation

Needs Assessment

It is important that planning the program be a collaborative process including input from:

- group members
- service providers to potential group members
- employers or work placement supervisors
- other agencies or those with expertise about student group.

"Felt" needs (expressed by participants) and "expressed" needs (which emerge throughout the course) can combine to ensure relevant program planning. Mary Beth Levan has presented a model of group needs and possible interventions (see Figure 21).

Sequencing of Lessons

In his paper, Paul Smith[1] suggests that there is a logical sequence for skill development, in which simple behaviours and sub-skills are subsumed by a higher order of complex skills. For example, many of the basic communications skills are pre-requisites for other skills and might be learned early in a training program. At the same time, elementary problem-solving and self-awareness skills are pre-requisites for more complex skills.

It is incumbent on the Life Skills coach to sequence lessons according to the needs of the students. Group members also identify personal issues as they arise and offer suggestions for lessons.

Continuous Intake and the DACUM Approach

As previously discussed, some typical topics for lessons can be anticipated by the Life Skills coach. At the same time, issues identified by group members can lead to development of lessons. Further, some Life Skills groups do not have a given start and finish date for all participants. In these settings, a new student joins an ongoing group as soon as a space becomes available. This is called "continuous intake". As a result, the traditional chronological curriculum approach is less applicable and makes the concept of sequencing lessons according to complexity of skills very challenging.

The DACUM (Design A Curriculum) approach allows a coach to draw up a tentative curriculum by preparing potential lesson topics. It allows for flexibility in the sequencing of the lessons and accommodates continuous intake. It permits group members the opportunity to identify specific personal subject areas as well.

---

[1]Paul Smith, *The Development of a Taxonomy of the Life Skills Required to Become a Balanced Self-Determined Person* (Employment and Immigration Canada, Occupational and Career Analysis and Development, 1981).

Need	Need Satisfied	Need Unsatisfied	Corrective Action
Sense of purpose	Feelings of unity, security and involvement Productive, self-initiating behaviour	Feelings of apathy and insecurity Inactivity, little initiative Group fragmentation	Be clear in affirming realistic goals with employers and group members
Leadership	Feelings of security. Focus on work. Trusting atmosphere. Organized approach to work.	Insecurity and feelings of fragmentation. Inconsistent behaviour.	Be honest, consistent and fair. Be receptive to feedback (not defensive). Work at maintaining appropriate group structures. Empower the group.
Environmental	Ability to focus on higher level needs Feelings of comfort and ease	Restless behaviour Sense of frustration and boredom	Plan environment of group carefully before group starts
Interpersonal	Feeling at ease Easy flow of discussion Interest in others grows Mutual support is evident Creative problem-solving evident	Feelings of insecurity Power struggles and withdrawn behaviour Evidence of impatience and boredom	Encourage mutual support and group problem-solving
Intrapersonal	Feelings of joy and contentment Congruent behaviour Openness and trust grow	Feelings of sadness and frustration Meeting needs in destructive methods - food, alcohol, quitting group, gossiping	Be sensitive - communicate directly with the individual Encourage expressiveness about real needs
Community Support	Feelings of belonging and validation from the larger community	Feelings of insecurity and disunity within the community or a "them and us" mentality Possible breakdown of group	Involve the community from the beginning in planning Invite appropriate community members to assist

Figure 21 Group Needs

The accompanying DACUM (see Figure 22) originally developed by Larry Sellon of St. Clair College in Windsor, Ontario and adapted for the Job Readiness Training program at George Brown College in Toronto in 1975, is an example of this approach. The five areas of Life Skills are identified and further broken down into sub-sections with potential lesson topics. The sequencing of lessons from simple to complex can be altered.

The competencies listed can be learned over the duration of a student's stay in the Life Skills program. Students can be given a copy of the proposed DACUM and can offer amendments as partners in the curriculum development and presentation of lessons.

Resources Required

Resources and materials vary from setting to setting. Budget constraints can put restrictions on the availability of resources. Some suggestions for resources might be:

- video-cassette player and monitor
- video-tape camera
- audio-tape recorder
- overhead projector
- flip-charts
- white and/or chalk board
- resource books for stimulus and skill practise activities
- pencils, non-toxic markers, masking tape, writing paper
- art supplies (paper, scissors, glue)
- magazines
- telephone
- child care provisions
- transit tickets/tokens
- kettle, coffee maker, mugs (if applicable)
- name tags

Ongoing Evaluation

Essential to the success of any Life Skills program is the need for ongoing evaluation of the program. The input, feedback and critique of the coach and the program from the participants and the community is a vital component of Life Skills programming. It

SELF		
Life Experience	Working with Others	Reasoning Skills
Who Am I	Meeting and Relating to Others	Analyzing Task
Personal Strengths & Weaknesses	Attending Behaviours	A Rational Approach to Problems
Values Exploration	Seeing Yourself as Others See You	Creative Behaviour
Describing Feelings	Expressing Trust in a Group	Solving Problems With a Group
Setting Personal Goals	Giving & Receiving Feedback	Exploring Complex Group & Personal Problems
	Speaking, Debating & Discussions	Evaluating Problem-Solving Skills

FAMILY		
The Human Condition	The Family and You	
Loneliness	Family Relationships	
Stigma	Health & Nutrition	
Rights & Responsibilities	Abortion & Family Planning	
The Money Trap	Life Styles	
Drugs and Health	Single Parent Family	
Birth & Death	Major Illness	
	Budgeting	
	Landlord & Tenant	

COMMUNITY
The Community and You
Community Resources
Voting & Citizens Rights
Police, Courts and Corrections
Income Tax
Community Groups
Social Change
Organizing for Community Improvement

JOB	
Vocational Exploration	Job Search Skills
Exploring Employment Related Values	Where Are the Jobs
Exploring Employment Preferences	The Application Form
Exploring Employment Skills and Weaknesses	The Resume & Letter of Acceptance
Exploring Skills Required for Specific Jobs	The Job Interview
Evaluating Employability	Role-Playing the Job Interview
Forms of Employment	Dry Run Job Interviews
Unions & Work	Application of Job Search Skills
Jobs in the Community	Evaluating & Acting on Results of an Interview
	Planning for a Career
	Keeping the Job

LEISURE
Free Time Activities
What is Leisure?
Sport Activities
Making Leisure Work for You
Relaxation
Enjoying Leisure
Producing Ideas for Leisure

Figure 22 Life Skills DACUM

is from this input that the coach and the agency can revise or update the Life Skills lessons and program to meet the needs of the members and of the community.

This evaluation can be done formally, through a structured evaluation tool at the end of a Life Skills program for overall feedback or informally throughout the training, to ensure that member needs are heard and acknowledged. Unit 8 offers details and samples of specific tools for evaluation.

Non-Completion of the Life Skills Program

Not all individuals who undertake Life Skills training complete the course. Illness, change of address, dissatisfaction with the training are some reasons for withdrawal.

There also arise situations where an individual is not managing within the training, for example, when there is an unsuitable match between the program and the individual's needs.

While students are encouraged to make informed choices regarding the suitability of the Life Skills program, sometimes the Life Skills coach must intervene.

Criteria for dismissal from a program exist in many Life Skills settings. These criteria may include physical violence, threatening behaviour or high absenteeism.

Completion of the Life Skills Program

Upon completion of the terms of the Life Skills programs, individuals can be given a certificate of achievement by the coach or the institution, in recognition of having fulfilled the pre-requisites of the program.

7.2 Format, Techniques and Materials for a Life Skills Coach

Format

The format used in Life Skills is a group work method that focuses on improving problem-solving skills. The small group can:

- allow for the practice of "simple" behaviours which can be used as building blocks for other more complex behaviours

- encourage the development of trust among members so that participants feel safe enough to try new behavioural styles

- provide opportunities for individual self-expression

- allow for the effective use of feedback

- be diverse in its composition

- be a microcosm of the larger society

- provide time for individual and group needs to be met

- be sub-divided into smaller groups to allow for more air-time and intimacy

Techniques

Coaches choose from a variety of techniques to facilitate learning. Patricia Cranton's book *Planning Instruction for Adult Learners*[2] provides a method of categorizing a variety of techniques under three headings.

- coach-centred
- interactive
- individualized

---

[2]Patricia A. Cranton, *Planning Instruction for Adult Learners* (Toronto, Ontario: Wall and Thompson, 1989). Adapted with permission.

Coach-Centred	Interactive	Individualized
Lecture • participants are passive • appropriate when used for a short time and combined with other techniques	**Large Group Discussion** • may be time-consuming • encourages student involvement	**Programmed Instruction** • very structured • students work at own pace • students receive extensive feedback
Questioning • invites feedback and evaluation - monitors student learning • encourages student involvement - stimulates reflection • may cause anxiety for some	**Small Group Discussion** • participants are involved • effective for cognitive and affective learning • encourages team work	**Modularized Instruction** • can be time-consuming • very flexible formats • students work at own pace
Modelling • illustrates an application of a skill or concept • helps participants understand their goal • students are passive	**Peer Teaching** • requires careful planning and monitoring • utilizes differences in student expertise • encourages student involvement • supports the Practise, Use, Teach (P.U.T.) Motto	**Independent Projects** • can be time-consuming • students are actively involved in learning • encourages independence and creativity
Visualization • encourages creative thinking • can be used to reshape reality • may cause anxiety for some	**Group Projects** • require careful planning, including evaluation techniques • encourage active participation and team work	**Computerized Instruction** • may involve considerable instructor-time or expense • can be very flexible • students work at own pace • does not address social skills
	Field or Work Placement • occurs in natural setting • students are actively involved • management and evaluation may be difficult	**Logs** • participants work at own level and pace • encourages independent thinking • may cause anxiety for some
	Laboratory • requires careful planning and evaluation • students actively involved in a realistic setting	**Learning Contracts** • can be time-consuming • participants are actively involved in process • encourage self-directed learning
	Simulations, Games and Warm-ups • provide practise of specific skills • produce anxiety for some students • active student participation	
	Role-Playing • effective in affective and psychomotor domains • provides "safe" place to practise new behaviour • active student participation	
	Case Study • provides exposure to realistic issues • encourages involvement by participants • may evoke strong emotions	

Figure 23 A Summary of Instructional Techniques

Figure 23 provides a summary of some techniques with some distinguishing features of each. Some of the approaches that are commonly used in a Life Skills group will be elaborated on in the following section:

Questioning Techniques
Role-Playing
The Case Method
Logs
The Learning Contract
Guided Imagery
Warm Ups

The bibliography at the end of the text offers more detailed descriptions of the above and other techniques. The section concludes with a discussion of how to choose appropriate techniques to achieve the goals of the lesson.

Questioning Techniques

The ability to ask good questions is an essential part of any learning situation. Questioning sometimes can imply doubting or challenging, but it always means requesting information to gain knowledge, seek clarification, establish facts, evaluate or perhaps just satisfy curiosity.

The coach as motivator, planner, group discussion leader, instructor, counsellor and evaluator is faced with the challenge of making learning effective and meaningful. To do this, it is necessary for both coach and student to develop questioning techniques to facilitate discussion and free expression of feelings and ideas.

As a means of directing and stimulating discussion, questioning is a fundamental technique for the Life Skills coach. Questions serve to:

• stimulate thinking and create motivation for learning

• encourage mental activity

• accumulate data and develop subject matter

- gain facts to enhance problem-solving

- provide a means of evaluating the progress of the group as a whole

- provide an indication of a student's understanding of course material

- provide a check for students on their progress

- clarify communication during a discussion

- guide, limit or change the focus of discussion

- strengthen or consolidate learning

Forms of Questions

There are two general forms of questions: the narrow and the broad (also referred to as closed and open).

The Narrow Question (Closed)
This form of question is one that can be answered with a "yes" or "no" response, for example: *Did you find this material interesting?* Generally speaking, a narrow question should be avoided, because it does not invite discussion. When it is used, the narrow question should be followed by: "Why?", "How?" or, "Where?", inviting further explanation.

The Broad Question (Open)
This form requires elaboration or exploration, for example: *What do you think of this case?* Broad questions take one of two forms: the **Direct Question** or the **Overhead Question**.

- **The Direct Question**
  The coach poses a question and then, after a pause, asks for a response from a specific person. *What are some ways of handling this situation? ...What would you do Alison?* Direct questions should be used sparingly, otherwise the discussion will turn to a question and answer period between coach and students. Direct questions tend to discourage continued creative thinking of the other participants. Once the question has been directed to one member of the group, the others may

be "off the hook" and need not necessarily continue to search for an answer.

- **The Overhead Question**
This technique involves asking a question of the group as a whole without mentioning anyone by name. For example: *What have we learned from this case?* The coach who uses this type of questioning can elicit more discussion from the group. A pause can be the most thought-provoking minute for all participants. The overhead question has many advantages if used skillfully. It stimulates mental activity, starts discussion and brings out different opinions.

Characteristics of Good Questions

Good questions usually have the following characteristics.

- **Challenge**
Stimulate the student to think: to relate, compare organize, evaluate and to draw inferences and conclusions. They should challenge an individual to apply knowledge rather than merely repeat facts.

    It is obvious that Marilda likes to work with Jyoti. What do you think some of the reasons are?

- **Brevity**
Include only the words needed to express the problem, yet be complete enough to eliminate the possibility of misunderstanding.

- **Clarity**
Stated in simple, straight-forward language.

    What did you learn from this lesson?

- **Relevance**
Have a definite purpose in mind. Trick questions should be avoided.

- **Emphasis on Major Points**
Build on the fundamental material in the lessons. Ask at the appropriate place in the lesson to emphasize key points.

We have identified a number of areas where we need more information before we can move ahead. What are the issues?

How to Use Questions

Good thought-provoking questions are a challenge to construct. It is sound practice to prepare questions on key points in advance of the lesson. One method is to identify the key points in the lesson, write the questions and incorporate them at the appropriate place in the lesson plan. Carefully prepared questions should not take the place of questions asked on the spur of the moment whenever it seems appropriate.

An effort should be made to fit the question to the individuals concerned; to keep questions appropriate to the level of the group; to use suitable terms if English is a second language.

Role-Playing

Role-playing is an effective technique which provides the participants with a supportive environment in which to rehearse and feel comfortable with new behaviour. By involving the "players" directly in situations which simulate their own life situations, the role-play ensures that learning is relevant. Role-play acts as the bridge between the group and the real world. It increases the likelihood that new behaviour will be adopted by building the individual's confidence and skill level. It has many uses in the Life Skills course including the development and support of balanced self-determined behaviour.

Objectives of Role Play

• increase insight and understanding

• facilitate the adoption of new behaviours

• provide a supportive mechanism for practising new skills

• provide opportunities to improve skills based on constructive feedback

- build confidence

How to Use Role-Play

Establish the ground rules

- confidentiality is to be honoured; personal situations should not be discussed outside of the group

- participants can stop the role-play at any time to ask for suggestions, feedback or support before resuming

- players can ask someone else to "fill in" for them; this gives them some ideas or help should they get stuck

- role-playing is optional

- acting ability is not important; the goal is to simulate real situations

Clarify Objectives

- group members and coach should all agree about the specific purpose of each role-play.

Prepare the Players

- players need to be clear about their roles

- participants can choose stage names to separate the player from the role (unless they choose to play themselves)

- imaginary scene is set

- a coach or shadow can be assigned for each player

Perform the Role-Play

- enough time is allotted for the role-play

- scenario ends when the energy level tapers off

- coach may intervene and make suggestions if players get stuck

Debrief the Players

- players are assisted in stepping out of the roles and resuming their own identities. Example: *What was it like playing that role?*

- players should be acknowledged for playing the roles

- participants are encouraged to analyze and extrapolate new learning from the role-play

Sample Debriefing Questions

Ask the role-players:

- *What did you like about your behaviour?*

- *What would you change?*

- *What was difficult?*

- *How did you feel during the role-play?*

- *What was effective about what the other player(s) said?*

- *What else might the other(s) have said?*

- *How did you react in this situation?*

Ask the group:

- *What were some examples of effective behaviour in this role-play?*

- *What suggestions would you make?*

- *What did you observe happening in the role-play?*

- *What have you learned from this role-play?*

Repeat the Role-Play if desired

- players can be asked to repeat the role-play in order to integrate any feedback they have received

- repetition is part of learning, not an indication of failure

Overcoming Resistance to Role-Playing

The following approaches can help to overcome initial anxieties:

- use a warm up exercise

- do role-plays in small groups

- allow participants to volunteer or choose roles randomly

- do not assign roles

- allow participants the right to choose when to do a role-play

- lead group members in deep breathing exercises or visualization techniques

- be positive about the benefits of role-playing

Types of Role-Play

Planned
The coach has specific goals, roles defined and situation pre-planned.

Scripted
The exact words are given by the coach or written by players.

Unscripted
Players say whatever seems appropriate.

Role-Reversal
The coach or another group member plays **A**'s role while **A** plays the role of the other person **B**. This provides **A** with the opportunity to experience the situation from the perspective of **B** and to see how another person would handle the situation. Roles may be reversed again for additional practice.

Role-rotation
A number of participants may share a role.
Example: Role-play responding to a difficult interview question. One member plays the employer, then each member takes a turn responding to the question.

Total Group
The coach presents a situation.
Example: A committee meeting to play an event in which all group members assume roles.

Coach Skills Required

The effective involvement of participants in role-play presumes the following coaching skills:

- demonstrate respect for others' feelings

- establish trust between coach and participants to facilitate risk-taking

- give clear instructions and set clear guidelines and boundaries

- model role-playing and receive and give both negative and positive feedback

- assess appropriateness of role-playing techniques to a particular participant or problem situation

- use role-play so that all involved see its direct relevance and value

- introduce role-play in a manner that prevents it from being perceived as gimmicky or silly

- demonstrate own level of personal comfort with role-playing

Role-Play Scenarios

Situations for role-play can be real or simulated.

Real Situations

- are brought by participants from their lives

- make a link between training and the real world to facilitate learning

- provide interest and motivation

- are specific and within the scope of the program

- can be emotionally charged

Mock or Simulated Situations

- can illustrate assertive principles involved in balanced self-determined behaviour

- are less emotional and therefore easier to practise

- warm up group to role-playing in a safe way

- provide stimulus for participants to think about related personal situations

- need to be socially and culturally relevant to the group[3]

The Case Method

The case method is a process in which the group considers a situation that could occur in life. It studies, analyzes and discusses the circumstances involved; it identifies the problems; it proposes possible solutions; and, with guidance, it organizes and evaluates the solutions proposed. It can be used as either a stimulus or a skill practise in a Life Skills Lesson.

---

[3]*Discovering Life Skills: Communicating Assertively - Volume VI* (YWCA of Metropolitan Toronto, 2nd Edition 1994), pp. 41-45.

A case study is brought into the classroom, where it can be considered without the actual risks and pressures which may accompany such problems in real life. It helps if participants are familiar with or can identify with the issues or values at stake.

The purpose of the case method is to facilitate both content and process.

Content

It is anticipated that the group members will apply their knowledge to a problem in a safe environment. They study, analyze and discuss the problem with their peers. They propose and evaluate solutions under the guidance of a coach. When and if they meet a similar problem in real life, they are be able to:

- recall some of the possible solutions discussed in class

- remember where they might go for expert advice, information or other help, if needed

- approach the problem more objectively because of having considered it before

Process

It is anticipated that, as a result of having worked the various steps in problem-solving, having had considerable practice in applying the steps and having engaged in much group discussion, the transfer of these skills will occur. In the future, group members will be able and likely to:

- solve problems in their lives more efficiently

- work with others

- participate more fully in community affairs

- talk and listen to others in such a way that real communication occurs

Case Format

A good case is suitable to the topic, length, mode of presentation and reading level of the group. It is simple enough that the discussion can focus on a few major points without having an obvious, easy solution. It is also reality-based making the situation more authentic.

There are various forms the case may take which may affect the ways in which it is presented.

Issue
Describes what happened up to a crucial point and then lets the group propose ways of coping with the situation.

Descriptive
Describes a situation including the way it was handled. Can be exciting if it is a current or controversial event.

Problem
Describes a case and lets the group decide whether there is a problem, what it is and how it might be solved.

Progressive
Is in two or more parts, each of which describes the situation up to a certain crucial point, then provides for discussion and suggestions as to what might or should happen next.

Why Use Case Studies?

Life Skills students find the case method an effective way of developing and improving their problem-solving skills. It provides an opportunity to practise:

- expressing thoughts in a group
- developing ideas in a logical sequence
- devising and evaluating solutions
- listening

The case method combines well with other methods, furnishing a vehicle for discussion, for problem-solving and for the examination of attitudes. It affords motivation for acquiring knowledge and an opportunity to apply it.

Strengths of the Case Method

Some advantages of the case method over, for instance, the lecture method are that it stimulates active participation and thus heightens interest. It de-emphasizes the "authority" and "fountain-of-knowledge" functions of the coach. It takes an open, questioning approach. It permits a true exchange of ideas and often leads to continuing thought on the topics discussed. Finally, it permits students to bring their life experience to bear on the subject, but lets them express it in relation to the person in the case study without revealing details of their own lives.

The case method is suitable when:

- the purpose is to give training and practice in effective problem-solving

- there is no obvious right answer

- students intend to apply their knowledge but may have difficulty in doing so

Limitations of the Case Method

The case method would not be suitable where:

- the subject matter is a definite set of facts to be learned

- time is limited and information is needed as quickly as possible

- students will have to meet a formal standard for achievement of knowledge or specific skills

- concepts, communication skills or language skills are not sufficiently developed to support a discussion

The Log

The log, sometimes referred to as a learning journal, is a written record of the student's learning process. It is a potentially creative and powerful teaching tool in that it:

- encourages participants to bridge the gap between what they learn in a Life Skills lesson and their personal life experience

- invites students, by enhancing their reflective skills, to develop connections between "knowing", "feeling" and "doing" in order to complete the learning cycle

- promotes awareness of change in oneself in terms of concrete observable behaviour, new thoughts, ideas and attitudes

- validates that reflecting and clarifying are sometimes most easily done alone

The learning process encouraged by the log is similar to the creative process. It provides an opportunity for participants to reflect and search for answers. It is an active process as opposed to a passive one. It equips students with the ability to think for themselves, allowing them to become more confident and self-directed. It is a technique that is new to many participants. It is critical that the coach helps establish a safe environment that is non-judgemental, accepting and encouraging of risk-taking. The goal is the development of a trusting relationship where the coach and student learn from each other. Log writing offers an opportunity for individuals to feel a sense of control over their thought processes.

If the log is to be shared with the coach, it offers an opportunity for dialogue - within oneself, between self and the content of a lesson or between self and the coach. The log can provide the student with an opportunity to give feedback to and receive feedback from the coach.

The style and length should allow for creativity and individual differences in learning styles. Some ideas for the format could include:

- stream of consciousness
- sentence completion statements
- audio tapes
- other art forms

Guidelines for Life Skills Logs

Sample questions to consider when writing a log:

WHAT I FELT ABOUT:

- myself?

- the way I participated? or didn't participate?

- others?

- things other people said?

- whether or not my needs were met?

- what happened; to me, in me, with others, around me?

- what did I like? dislike?

- what happens to me in the group?

- what physical manifestations did I have and what connections can I make with what might have been happening to me emotionally?

WHAT I LEARNED ABOUT:

- myself?

- other people?

- through the exercise(s)?

- values and what is important to me?

- strengths that I recognize within myself?

- how was I empowered by what I learned today?

- skills that were new to me?

WHAT I WILL DO:

- for myself?

- about things that still puzzle me?

- to enhance my goals/learning contract?

- who might I contact to learn more about?

- what resources do I have available to me now to further my learning?

- what is my next step?

The Learning Contract

A learning contract is a document which outlines a student's plan for learning. Research[4] on adult learning indicates that when adults learn something (as contrasted with being taught) on their own initiative, they learn more deeply and permanently.

Learning contracts can be used to negotiate and problem-solve issues that arise when there is a difference between the needs and expectations of a Life Skills program and those of the participant. The process is similar to problem-solving and goal setting. Hence, developing learning contracts helps to reinforce those skills that are central in a Life Skills program.

Contract learning can be undertaken between a participant and the coach, a work placement supervisor or peers. The process includes:

- identifying needs: for example, the gap between where the individuals are now and where they want to be

- designing a list of the competencies required to perform the task: for example, the ability to be a good listener involves a number of competencies that can be listed. The next task is to

---

[4]Allen Tough, *The Adult's Learning Projects* (Toronto: Ontario Institute for Studies in Education, 1971).

assess the gap between where they are now and where they want to be in regard to each competency

- setting objectives - setting an objective for each of the needs to be worked on as assessed in step 1

- identifying resources and strategies - describing how learners propose to go about accomplishing their goals or objectives

- identifying evidence and validation for achievements - describing what evidence participants will use to indicate the degree to which they have achieved each objective

- reviewing the contract with others involved - asking others to get their reactions and suggestions

- implementing the contract - doing what the contract calls for and revising as needed

- evaluating the learning - assessing how much is accomplished and what the next steps are

By participating in the whole process, the learners develop a sense of ownership and commitment to the plan.

Visualization

Visualization, sometimes referred to as guided imagery, is a useful and powerful technique that can be used to achieve a variety of educational objectives. It can be used to:

- enhance self-esteem
- expand awareness and creativity
- facilitate optimal performance of a skill
- encourage positive thinking

Creative visualization involves the use of the imagination to reshape or create what one wants in life. By repeated visualization, using positive energy, the vision created is steadily reinforced until it becomes a reality. It involves picturing oneself as if the desired outcome has already happened, thus creating an inner experience of what it would be like to have one's desire come true.

Visualization takes many forms. Some people actually see an image; others experience a sense or general feeling of the image. Visualization improves with practise. It is important to introduce guided imagery to your participants with a rationale for its use and some short engaging visualizations to encourage group discussion. The following tips are a guide to prepare participants.

- To help participants feel peaceful they can be directed to take some deep breaths or find a relaxed position.

- Usually, participants do visualizations with their eyes closed; some are more comfortable with their eyes open.

- It is important to pay attention to the climate of the room by creating a safe space, dimming the lights and using quiet music to block out "white noise".

- Participants may fall asleep during a visualization.

- Group members need permission to go off on their own if drawn to do so. That may be more helpful to the individual.

- Other participants need encouragement to practise having control over their images and may want to keep refocusing each time their mind wanders off.

- Images are not compared or judged by others.

- Verbal sharing after the visualization is a matter of choice.

- Give permission to students to set their own boundaries in relation to the depth they choose to go into.

- Participants are often encouraged to write or draw something following a visualization exercise.

- Allow time to bring students back to a normal waking consciousness. This can be done by slowly counting to the number five or by allowing each individual to become conscious of the sounds, feel of the space around them and to slowly open their eyes when they are ready.

- Participants need to discover their own meanings for their symbols and images knowing that the message may emerge after some reflection.

Sample Visualizations

The following are two short exercises to introduce visualization. Many visualizations are longer and may take up to 20 minutes, with additional time for debriefing. Refer to the bibliography for additional sources on visualization.

Sample I:
Imagine that someone has just given you a big slice of lemon and you have bitten into it. You can taste the tart, sour lemony taste. You can feel the juice on your lips...[5]

Sample II:
Imagine that you are lying on a beach by the ocean...You hear the waves and the wind and some birds calling...You feel the warmth of the sun...the sand under your body...The gentle breeze on your skin...Your breathing is in tune with the rise and fall of the waves...[6]

Warm Ups

A 'Warm Up' is the general term used to describe short activities that may be used at various points in the lesson.

Types of warm ups include climate setters, energizers and inclusion exercises. They help focus group members on the "here and now". Warm ups can be used to warm-up, cool-down, motivate, stimulate or encourage a change of pace of the group. They can be relaxing or action-oriented and may or may not be related to the topic of a lesson.

One thing that any warm up should do is provide a safe non-judgemental environment for group members which will encourage participation and sharing.

---

[5]*Discovering Life Skills, Volume VI* (YWCA of Metropolitan Toronto, 2nd Edition 1994), p. 230.

[6]Ibid., p. 231.

Warm Up Ideas

Sample exercises can be grouped together under headings such as:

I Climate Setters
These are useful to set the tone at the beginning of a session.

II Inclusion exercises
These help group members discover their commonalities and to foster group cohesiveness.

III Energizers
These can be used to change the pace or stimulate a group.

IV Closers
These are suitable for bringing a session to closure.

V Relaxers
These can be used to relieve stress, anxiety or focus a group on the here and now.

5WHs of Designing or Choosing a Warm Up

There are a number of considerations to keep in mind when designing or choosing warm ups.

Who?
For whom is the warm up appropriate?
Consideration must be given to ages, abilities, cultural backgrounds, type of group.

Who chooses the warm up?
Group members can take on the responsibility of preparing and facilitating this as well as the coach.

Why?
Why choose this warm up?
The goal is to warm up, energize, sensitize, focus, stimulate, build cohesion.

When?
When would you use this warm up?

Sometimes it is appropriate for early sessions or toward the end of a course when people are better acquainted.

Within a group session, an exercise might be more suitable at the beginning, ending or as an energizer in the middle.

Where?
Where is the warm up being done?
Consider the size of the room and the use of alternative facilities such as adjoining rooms or a gym.

What?
What do you need to do to be prepared for the unexpected?
It is helpful to have a Life Skills coach's 'Bag of Tricks' (a selection of objects and memorabilia that can be used on the spot).

Examples

- a clock: "I remember a time when..."

- a book: "My favourite hero is..." or "If I were writing my autobiography, the title would be..."

- a key: Pass around to see how many uses can be found

Refer to the bibliography for additional resources

How?
How can one be more creative? Get new ideas?

Working on developing creativity takes some effort. The following points may help:

- change of perception (look at things in different ways)

- exercise the mind (do puzzles, quizzes)

- read 'creativity' books

- network (borrow or share ideas with others)

- ask the group if they have any games or ideas they could contribute

Summary: Choosing Appropriate Techniques

A Life Skills coach is confronted with the task of choosing the best technique to accomplish the goals of the lesson. Malcolm Knowles, in his book *The Modern Practice of Adult Education*, notes that the ability to select the most effective technique for a specific purpose is likely best developed through experience and ongoing evaluation. Knowles suggests that two simple guidelines may help in making a choice:

- match the technique to the objective (see Figure 24).

- given a choice, choose the technique involving the group members in the most active participation

Materials

Today's world is filled with materials and devices that can expand when, where and how we learn. Ideally, a Life Skills program makes use of a variety of materials to create a rich learning environment. The goal is to stimulate participants to learn and develop skills that are significant and related to their goals. Posters, books, computers, pamphlets, bulletin boards, audio and video tapes can be helpful in accessing information and expanding the learning options. The selection and use of materials is a complex and rapidly changing aspect of teaching/coaching. It is beyond the scope of this book to examine all the options in detail. The bibliography listed at the back of this book offers many resources. The following generalizations however, may be helpful in making some decisions about materials to use in a Life Skills group.

Printed Materials

- provide the most portable, flexible way for providing and gathering information

- require that the participant be an effective reader

- present a serious obstacle for many learners

Type of Behavioural Outcome	Most Appropriate Technique
Knowledge (generalizations about experience; internalization of information)	lecture, television, debate, dialogue, interview, symposium, panel, group interview, colloquium, motion picture, slide film, recording, book-based discussion, reading
Understanding (application of information and generalization)	audience participation, demonstration, motion picture, dramatization, Socratic discussion, problem-solving discussion, case study, critical incident process, games
Skills (incorporation of new ways of performing through practice)	role playing, in-basket exercises, games, action mazes, participative case, T-Group, nonverbal exercises, skill practice exercises, drill, coaching
Attitudes (adoption of new feelings through experiencing greater success with them than with old)	experience-sharing discussion, group-centred discussion, role playing, critical incident process, case study games, participative cases, T-Group, nonverbal exercises
Values (the adoption and priority arrangement of beliefs)	television, lecture (sermon), debate, dialogue, symposium, colloquium, motion picture, dramatization, guided discussion, experience-sharing discussion, role playing, critical incident process, games, T-Group
Interests (satisfying exposure to new activities)	television, demonstration, motion picture, slide film, dramatization, experience-sharing discussion, exhibits, trips, nonverbal exercises

Figure 24 Matching Techniques to Desired Behavioural Outcomes

Audio-Visual Aids

- offer alternatives to reading for those who have difficulty with written materials

- are useful for visual and auditory learners

- provide variety

- provide access to large pools of information

- provide flexibility in timing to meet needs of individual students

- require monitoring and maintenance of equipment

- incur costs

The Life Skills coach as an adult educator has to be constantly assessing the learning styles and needs of participants and adapting materials to maximize the students' learning.

Edgar Dale's classic model[7] seen in Figure 25 indicates the types of materials best suited to a variety of ways of grasping information. It gives the Life Skills coach some ideas about matching materials to the learning styles and preferences of their participants.

It is important to recognize that the cone does not imply a value hierarchy, that one level is better than another or that direct experience should be substituted for indirect experience. Dale does maintain that *you can use indirect experiences wisely and well only when they are built on direct experiences.*[8]

Materials and What They Communicate

The print and visual materials which surround and support individuals in a Life Skills program communicate a wide range of

---

[7]Edgar Dale, *Audio-Visual Methods in Teaching* (New York: Dryden Press, 1954), p. 43.

[8]Ibid., p. 99.

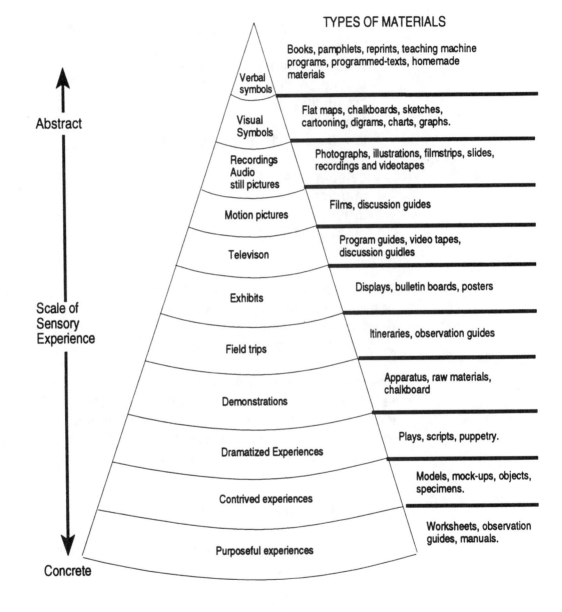

TYPES OF MATERIALS

Books, pamphlets, reprints, teaching machine programs, programmed-texts, homemade materials

Verbal symbols

Visual Symbols

Flat maps, chalkboards, sketches, cartooning, digrams, charts, graphs.

Recordings Audio still pictures

Photographs, illustrations, filmstrips, slides, recordings and videotapes

Motion pictures

Films, discussion guides

Televison

Program guides, video tapes, discussion guidles

Exhibits

Displays, bulletin boards, posters

Field trips

Itineraries, observation guides

Demonstrations

Apparatus, raw materials, chalkboard

Dramatized Experiences

Plays, scripts, puppetry.

Contrived experiences

Models, mock-ups, objects, specimens.

Purposeful experiences

Worksheets, observation guides, manuals.

Abstract

Scale of Sensory Experience

Concrete

Figure 25 Edgar Dale's Cone of Experience

messages about the world we live in.[9] They express ideas about:

- who is important and who is not

- what is "normal" and "abnormal"

- what are significant issues and what are not

- what are acceptable practices in:
  - raising children
  - community life
  - family life
  - language and communication
  - sexuality
  - celebrations
  - nutrition
  - dress
  - problem-solving
  - work

These messages both reflect particular ways of thinking and perceiving and shape the way we see ourselves and others. They have a strong impact on the relationships we develop and on the understandings of how our society works.

Images and content are never neutral. They are necessarily selective; in their selectivity, they elevate certain ideas and diminish others. The questions for programs are which ideas and images must be central to communications and which ideas and images should be de-emphasized.

Criteria for Assessing and Creating Program Materials

The following questions are intended to assist with assessing and creating materials.

- Is there bias by omission?
  (Does the picture or text include representation of all societal group members as a natural and unremarkable part of the

---

[9]Barb Thomas, *Multiculturalism at Work: A Guide to Organizational Change* (Toronto: YWCA of Metropolitan Toronto, 1987), p. 91.

scene or situation?)

- Is there bias by disparagement?
(Are certain non-mainstream groups visually or verbally depicted as "comic" or less worthy of respect, because they differ in some particular way from the majority in appearance or practice?)

- Is there bias by distortion of fact?
(Do pictures inaccurately depict physical characteristics and skin tones, whether through careless printing or through intent. Do descriptions or stories tell only one side of the situation or uses value-laden language to describe the actions of one group?)

- Is there a bias by tacit assumption?
(Are minority group members shown only in secondary, never in leadership roles; always in blue-collar, never in white-collar jobs; as peripheral rather than central characters or actors.)

It is a major challenge to eliminate all expressions of bias. It is important to recognize that it is possible to make the materials used in a program acceptable to all of its constituency. The following tip sheet is provided as another tool for assessment of materials.[10] There may be other indicators and issues you wish to add to the list.

---

[10]Ibid., p. 148.

Issues to Consider	What Does This Material Communicate?
1. ILLUSTRATIONS Who is included? What are they doing?	
2. STORY/NARRATIVE LINE Standards of success. Methods for resolution of problems? Role of diverse groups?	
3. LIVES AND EXPERIENCES Assumptions? Contrasts and comparisons? Is it accurate?	
4. RELATIONSHIPS Who has the power to do what? Depiction of family composition?	
5. HEROES (Masculine and Feminine) Whose heroes? Whose interests do they represent? Depiction of age, gender, sexual orientation, class?	
6. LANGUAGE English and/or other? Words describing people?	
7. PERSPECTIVE Whose voices? What perspective?	
8. RESOURCES SUGGESTED Focus? Whose issues are addressed?	
9. ACTIVITIES SUGGESTED Cultural compatibility? Conflicts frankly examined?	
10. EFFECTS ON READER/USER How is the material affirming? How does it stretch possibilities?	

Figure 26 Assessing Program Materials

8

Evaluation

8.1 Rationale

Evaluation is an integral part of the Life Skills model. To evaluate is to determine the **value** of the program. The central question in an evaluation is the degree to which the program has met its objectives. Was the program effective?

Evaluation is important for all of the players in the Life Skills program: for the Life Skills coach (to assess if the program is meeting participant needs); for the participants (to assess progress towards their learning goals); and for the community (to assess if the program has met community needs).

Evaluation is sometimes ignored or given a low priority in many programs, including Life Skills programs. Some of the barriers to evaluation are:

- lack of time and/or money

- lack of knowledge about how to conduct an evaluation

- previous negative experiences with evaluations

- discomfort with giving and receiving feedback

- difficulty of measuring changes in behaviour, attitude, quality of life

- extensive evaluation not required by sponsoring agency

- fear of results not measuring up to expectations

There are several different levels of evaluation. The basic questions the evaluation is required to answer are:

- How did participants experience the program? (REACTION)

- What did participants learn? (LEARNING)

- How did the learning translate into changed behaviour in the "real world"? (BEHAVIOUR)

- Did the program have the desired impact? (RESULTS)
  (Or did the program meet all of its objectives?)

8.2   The Life Skills Philosophy of Evaluation

Evaluating programs, particularly programs that deal with personal development, attitude or behaviour change, is a complex and difficult task. Human behaviour is difficult to quantify. Tests that are reliable and valid measures of behaviour are difficult to find. Research in the area of behaviour change (for example, in assertiveness studies), yield conflicting results.

Malcolm Knowles, a well-know expert in the field of adult education, writes that evaluation has become *a much over-emphasized sacred cow* and therefore is a source of confusion, frustration and guilt for educators.[1] The rigorous, scientific approach to evaluation of personal development programs is not always feasible or useful.

Life Skills favours a learner-centred versus a teacher-centred method of evaluation. In a Life Skills program, the locus of responsibility is with the learners to evaluate the program and their learning in the program. Self-evaluation, as opposed to evaluation by the coach is the method of choice. Figure 27

---

[1]Malcolm Knowles, *The Modern Practice of Adult Education* (New York: Association Press, 1976), p. 219.

illustrates the difference between the two approaches to evaluation.[2]

	Teacher-Centred	Learner-Centred
Goals	Educating Making changes in person	Facilitating change Providing resources for self-directed inquiry and self-development
Rationale	Efficiency - maximum change in the shortest time at minimum cost	Help participants assess whether their objectives were met Learn the skill of evaluation
Purpose	Quantification	Involvement
Methods	Standardized tests Instructor-designed measures of learning and performance	Collaborative planning of evaluation methods May include tests devised by students to measure objectives Feedback from peers and facilitator

Figure 27 Teacher-Centred versus Learner-Centred Evaluation

---

[2]*Discovering Life Skills, Volume V* (Toronto: YWCA of Metropolitan Toronto, 1994), p. 198.

The rationale for self-evaluation is imbedded in the philosophy and methodology of Life Skills. A Life Skills program is learner-centred, addressing the expressed and felt needs of the learners. The methodology is participatory, democratic and inclusive. The coach is a guide versus an expert. Participants learn through structured exercises and through feedback from the group. While feedback from the group and the coach are important, the best judge of one's own learning is the individual person. Individuals set their own standards and aim to achieve their personal best.

Self-evaluation does not imply a haphazard method where individuals are left to their own devices to evaluate their learning. The Life Skills coach can provide the tools to assist participants to assess their progress and the effectiveness of the program in meeting their needs.

8.3   Planning for Evaluation: A Checklist

Plan the approach to evaluation by thinking through the following checklist:[3]

- What questions are to be answered? How did participants feel about the program? What did they learn? How did the training affect their attitudes and behaviour? What were the results in and outside of the group?

- How will items addressed in the questions be measured? What methods will be used?

- What are the objectives of the program? Are the evaluation criteria based on these objectives?

- How do the criteria relate to the needs expressed by the participants?

- What are the best and most cost-effective methods for measuring the results of the training?

---

[3] *Essentials for Evaluation* (Alexandria, Virginia: American Society for Training and Development, Info-Line Collection #8601, 1993).

- What data is required for the sponsor or funder?

- Who will be involved in conducting the evaluation?

- Have you explained the purpose of evaluation to the students and assured them of confidentiality?

8.4 The 5WHs of Evaluation

The 5WHs will serve to define the elements of an evaluation system. The questions WHO, WHY, WHEN, WHAT, WHERE and HOW are discussed in detail in the following sections.

Who?

Participants are the primary source of evaluation. Participants evaluate:

- the coach

- the individual Life Skills exercises and lessons

- the Life Skills program

- their learning throughout and after the course

Coaches also have a role to play in the evaluation system. Coaches evaluate:

- their own facilitation style and interventions

- the effectiveness of the exercises, lessons and overall program, based on feedback from participants

- the progress of the learning group

Community may also require an evaluation. Life Skills programs do not operate in a vacuum. They are often sponsored or mandated by an agency organization or funder. The community evaluates:

- the program's contribution to meeting a community need

- cost-benefit of the program

Why?

Evaluation is an essential component of any training program. The evaluation component of a Life Skills program determines if it has been effective in meeting its objectives. When evaluation is conducted in an ongoing way in a program, the lessons can be modified to meet the learning needs of participants. Evaluation also ensures that the program is constantly changing and adapting to changing needs in the community.

There is increasing pressure from funders and sponsors in time of shrinking financial resources to know if a program works and why they should continue to fund it. The Life Skills program is often required to come up with facts and figures to justify a program. The sections on WHAT and HOW will serve to assist Life Skills coaches in providing the answers to the question: Did the program accomplish its purpose?

Evaluation encourages the students to develop the skill of critical thinking, an essential skill in the problem-solving process. Self-evaluation requires the students to define their learning needs and to take some responsibility for getting their needs met. Awareness of needs and goals is essential in the learning process.

In summary, evaluation is important because:

- coaches need feedback to improve their style and learn what is effective and what is not

- participants gain practise in giving feedback

- promotes total participation in the design of the program

- it allows expression of feelings about group process

- it gives an opportunity to develop the skills for critical analysis

- it increases awareness for both participants and the coach of how people learn in different ways

- it provides evidence of effectiveness of the program to funders and sponsors

When?

Program evaluation begins even before the start of the program. Evaluation methods and questions will be based on needs assessments and program objectives. It is therefore necessary to plan the evaluation strategy in advance of the program. What are the needs to be addressed? What are the program objectives? The answers to these questions provide the criteria for evaluation.

Evaluations are conducted at various times during (and after) the Life Skills program.

Ongoing

This helps to ensure that the program is meeting the needs of the participants.

Examples:

Formal
- questionnaires

- round robin (for example, each student in turn around the room completes the sentence *one thing I learned today is...* or, *A lightbulb that came on for me was....*

- check-in (for example, *What assertive skills did you practice during the week? What worked and what didn't work?*)

Informal
- coach asks for feedback from the group (for example, *I notice the group is quiet today. What is happening?*)

- spontaneous remarks made by participants

At the end of each lesson

Evaluation is part of the Life Skills lesson design. It follows the application stage of the lesson. In the application phase, the questions asked are:

- *How can you use what you have learned today?*

- *What will you do differently or continue to do as a result of what we have reviewed today?*

In the evaluation phase of the lesson, the questions asked are:

- *What worked well? What could have been done differently?*

- *What was your experience in the lesson?*

- *Were the goals/objectives of the lesson met?*

- *What did you learn?*

Mid-way evaluation or periodic evaluation

It is important to take a reading of the group and its progress mid-way through a program, at certain intervals throughout the program or at points where it is obvious that the group does not appear to be functioning very well.

The mid-way evaluation could take many forms: written, verbal, round robin, informal discussion or structured discussion.

At the end of the program

When a program is ending, the evaluation is a summary of reaction, learning, behaviour and results. Students at this time are given the opportunity to assess in detail the impact of the program on their learning.

Follow-up (where possible)

Follow-up is desirable to help assess the long-term impact of learning and behaviour change. Follow-up evaluation is sometimes required by funders. The questions asked at this point will depend on the goals and objectives of the program. For example, if the Life Skills program was geared to employment, criteria for evaluation would be success in finding a job or entering a training or retraining program. If the Life Skills program was offered through a criminal justice agency, the criteria for success might be reduction of recidivism.

While objective criteria (statistics regarding jobs, recidivism) yield useful information, it is important also to consider other outcomes of a program and include questions to address these outcomes. These might include: communication skills, problem-solving skills, assertiveness, relationship skills and self-esteem.

A Life Skills program addresses "quality of life" issues. It is difficult to measure quality of life or the "soft skills" such as interpersonal skills. And yet these are the skills that lead to life satisfaction and success in any environment, including the workplace. While objective criteria may not be available to measure the "soft skills", follow-up questionnaires or interviews where participants self-evaluate, can provide evidence of learning in the areas of interpersonal communication, problem-solving and critical thinking.

In Life Skills, the method to assess skills acquisition, abbreviated as P.U.T. (practise, use, teach), is the measure by which skills integration can be evaluated as being successful.

What?

Evaluation is focused on the program content and it's delivery (coach and methods). Was it effective in meeting the goals and objectives? In Life Skills, the process or means of achieving the goals through the group is also evaluated. Both content and process evaluations will be addressed below.

Content

There are four components of an evaluation strategy to address the key question about content: Did the program meet overall goals? The components are:

Reaction
Learning
Behaviour
Results[4]

Figure 28 outlines the four components. Each provides different kinds of information that can help the determine the effectiveness of the Life Skills lessons or program. The various methods of conducting evaluations are addressed in the HOW section. Samples of the different kinds of evaluations can be found at the conclusion of this unit.

Reaction

A reaction type of evaluation determines how the participants experienced the program. Students give their reaction (verbally or in a questionnaire) to individual exercises, lessons, the course content in general, format, the facilitator's style, physical facilities and methods used.

The reaction type of evaluation gives the coach a quick reading of the opinions of students about the learning experience. It allows participants to have input on the various aspects of the program. When participants are having a favourable experience, they are more inclined to attend, participate and learn.

In designing a reaction evaluation it is important to:

- know what information is being sought, (for example, interest in topic, appropriateness of techniques, effectiveness of coach, adequacy of content)

- design an evaluation form using check marks and boxes or a rating scale to facilitate tabulating results

- establish a standard by converting a reaction to a number; for

---

[4]Dr. Donald L. Kirkpatrick, Techniques for Evaluating Training Programs, in *Training and Development Journal* (Madison, Wisconsin: American Society for Training and Development, 1978).

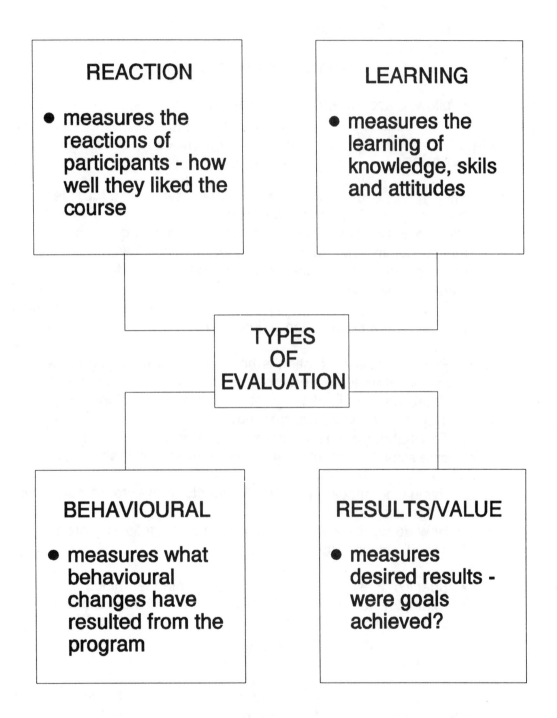

Figure 28 Types of Evaluation

example, a rating scale with numbers: 1 needs improvement, 2 adequate 3 good, 4 very good, 5 excellent

- keep the form simple

- make the forms anonymous to encourage honesty

- allow space for additional comments

Learning

This type of evaluation measures what new knowledge, ideas, concepts, principles and techniques the learner has acquired. While observations of the coach and feedback from group members can contribute to an understanding of what learning has occurred, the method used primarily in Life Skills to assess learning is self-evaluation.

In designing an evaluation of learning:

- Pre- and post-evaluation is helpful, preferably using some form of quantitative measurement, such as a scale from 1 to 10. What were the knowledge and skills at the beginning of the program and what are they now? To what degree have needs articulated in the needs assessment been met through the lesson/program?

- Evaluation should address all aspects of the stated objectives of the program. How do participants rate their skills in the following areas: assertiveness, problem-solving?

- Specific questions are asked to determine learning. Example: Name one skill you have learned that can be useful in the workplace? Why?

Behaviour

This level of evaluation addresses the change in behaviour during the program (both in the classroom and in the "real" world), resulting from new knowledge or skills. Do students have the motivation and ability to use the learning in "real-life" situations?

Behaviour can change only when:

- there is a will to do so

- there is a recognition for the need to change

- there is support and encouragement during the process

- there are opportunities to try to out the new behaviour (for example, in role plays, simulations, real-life)

When designing an evaluation for behaviour change

- pre and post measures are desirable

- self-evaluation and feedback from the group will enhance the evaluation (for example, students could rate each other on the "How I See Myself Now" scale)

- the evaluation ideally takes place at intervals throughout the program, at the end of the program and after a period of time following the program

Results

This type of evaluation refers to the extent to which the original purpose for the course was achieved? What will be the impact of the course on participants in their daily lives? Did the program accomplish its objectives? Was the impact of the program adequate for the amount of effort and expense?

The results or impact are the most difficult to measure because Life Skills coaches do not always have the means nor expertise to conduct follow-up studies.

Sometimes, an independent researcher is hired by the sponsor to conduct research on the results of a program. Typically, this kind of research uses scientific or quasi-scientific methods to study the short-term and longer-term outcomes of a program and its cost effectiveness.

For example, one research study conducted on a program for sole-support mothers, collected a variety of data to determine the impact of the program.[5] The data included:

- participants' perceptions of their experience in the program (through detailed interviews).

- changes in the participants' lives in the areas of self-esteem, goal setting, interpersonal relationships, academic skills and life management skills (through detailed interviews, observations of program workers, a self-esteem scale and tests for academic level).

- the cost-benefit of the program (through statistics on the number of women entering training/upgrading or finding employment and a cost/savings analysis).

While the above research was extensive, researchers still admit the difficulty of interpreting results with any certainty. The reasons include the lack of a comparison group, relatively short-term follow-up and the difficulty of quantifying life management self-esteem and interpersonal skills. It is very difficult to show through research, a direct chain effect of learning in the group and subsequent changes in behaviour in and outside of the group.

Follow-up interviews can, however, yield useful information for improvement of a program and for a general indication of how participants have applied their learning.

In designing an evaluation for results

- input from others can be helpful

- follow-up questionnaires, phone calls or interviews can help determine the effectiveness over time of the Life Skills program

- it is ideal to choose an outside evaluator with no vested interest in the outcome

- time, expertise and financial cost must be considered

[5]*Focus on Change Evaluation*, Revised Edition (Ontario: Ministry of Community and Social Services, Research Section, August 1981).

Process: Group Growth

Another area for the coach and participants to evaluate is the contribution of the group process to the achievement of individual and group goals. As Life Skills is based on a group method, the role of group dynamics in the learning process must be taken into consideration.

While the development of a group is not generally measured in quantifiable terms, it is important for the coach to reflect on the process of the group. It is also critical to obtain feedback from the group on how they see the group functioning and whether it is hindering or enhancing learning.

Some of the questions for the coach to consider are:

- What stage of development is the group in?

- What are the participation patterns?

- What is the energy level of the group?

- How dependent is the group on the leader?

For a more in-depth analysis on group dynamics and stages of group development, refer to Unit 5.

Questions for the participants would address their perception of the group including an evaluation of the following:

- communication channels

- resolving conflict

- group climate

- trust and safety

- productivity of group

- problem-solving

- teamwork

The above areas can be addressed in group discussion, questionnaire format or action methods. There are sample questionnaires at the conclusion of this unit that address participants views of group effectiveness. An example of an action method might be an exercise where participants pin a card on their shirts with three words to describe the group. They then circulate, without speaking, to see how others have described the group. Participants then discuss their observations in the large group.

It is important when looking at the process of a group to note that not all the stages of a group are experienced positively by participants. This does not necessarily mean that the group is not effective. It can be healthy for groups to have conflict, to have times of "storming", to have different opinions on preferred learning methods and to differ on group and individual goals. However, these group dynamics, when processed well, can lead to significant learning for individuals. Thus, some participants will say that they did not always enjoy the group experience but that they learned a great deal. It is therefore important in evaluations of group process to focus on the learning of participants rather than a qualitative measure of "enjoyment" of the group.

Where?

Evaluation of both content and group process take place in a variety of locations including:

- in the classroom (through discussion, questionnaires, etc)

- outside of the classroom (pre and post interviews, logs, questionnaires)

- informal discussion

The method used will largely determine the location of the evaluation. Because the focus is on self-evaluation in Life Skills, participants will draw on any number of scenarios and environments they are involved in before, during and after the Life Skills course to evaluate their progress in areas that are important to them.

How?

There are a number of methods to evaluate the effectiveness of the Life Skills program. The method used will depend upon the central question asked in the evaluation - or the type of evaluation one is conducting. Figure 29 lists some methods appropriate to different types or approaches to evaluation.

Approaches to Evaluation	Methods of Evaluation
Reaction: measures reactions How did you experience the course? exercise? lesson? session?	• ask questions • questionnaires • interviews • group discussion • action sociogram
Learning: measures skills, knowledge, attitude What did you learn?	• quiz, test • role play • simulation, games • written exercises
Behavioural: measures changes in behaviour What will you do differently? How can you apply this learning to make changes in behaviour? What behavioural changes can you identify - in group, outside the group?	• questionnaires • behavioural assessments • observation • interviews • action plays
Results: measures overall objectives Were the objectives achieved? Were your expectations met? What was the impact of the training in your home/work environment?	• follow up • successes out of group • questionnaires • phone calls • testimonials

Figure 29 Evaluation Theory

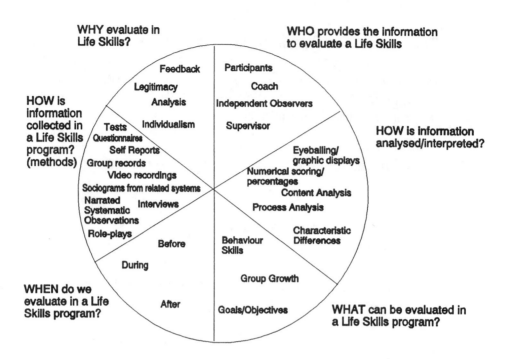

Figure 30 Summary: An Evaluation Strategy

8.5 Sample Evaluations

In the following section are examples of evaluations used to assess both the content (reaction, learning, behavioural, results) and the process of a group. To encourage honest reactions, participants have the option of signing their names or not.

Many of the sample evaluations assess the program at more than one level; they may look at reaction and learning or learning and behaviour or other combinations. Some use sophisticated language and some do not; some are detailed and others are meant to be filled out spontaneously.

It is important to consider the language and needs of the group in designing evaluations. There are methods for evaluation other than paper and pencil questionnaires, including group discussion and action methods.

Some examples of action methods are:

• Yeah - Boo cards: Coach distributes 2 placards to each participant, one with Yeah written on it and one with BOO. Coach asks the members to evaluate various components of the lesson by raising the appropriate placard.

• Critical Mass: Participants in small groups build a "statement" of their feelings about the session. Materials can include construction paper, crepe paper, markers scissors, paper cups, playdough and other creative material.

• Message to the World: Participants are asked to prepare a skit, poem, play or other creative method to demonstrate to the rest of the group what they have learned in the course.

Whatever the method, creativity in design and openness to the results can lead to valuable information for the group, coach, agency and community.

The evaluations included in this section are:

Evaluation	Type
1. Program evaluation	Reaction
2. Feedback sheet	Reaction
3. Mid-way evaluation	Reaction
4. Evaluation of sessions	Reaction/Learning
5. Lesson evaluation	Reaction /Learning
6. Group behaviour inventory	Behavioural/Group Process
7. Group evaluation form	Reaction/Learning/Behavioural/ Process
8. General evaluation survey	Reaction/Learning
9. Evaluation: one thing	Learning
10. Evaluation: a snapshot	Learning/Behavioural
11. Lesson evaluation form	Reaction/Learning/Behavioural
12. How I see myself now	Learning/Behavioural/Results
13. Checklist for the coach	

1. Program Evaluation

Please rate the following by circling the appropriate number on the scale below:

Overall Rating of the Program:

10	9	8	7	6	5	4	3	2	1
Excellent									Needs Work

Content:

10	9	8	7	6	5	4	3	2	1
Excellent									Needs work

Coach(es):

10	9	8	7	6	5	4	3	2	1
Excellent									Needs work

Handling Questions:

10	9	8	7	6	5	4	3	2	1
Excellent									Needs work

Participant Handouts:

10	9	8	7	6	5	4	3	2	1
Excellent									Needs work

Facilities:

10	9	8	7	6	5	4	3	2	1
Excellent									Needs work

2. Feedback

3. Mid-way Evaluation

1. How would you describe your involvement and participation in these sessions? (Circle the appropriate number).

1   2   3   4   5   6   7   8   9   10

Uninvolved   Very Involved

2. What has been your reaction to the sessions thus far? In what ways does the group meet your needs?

3. How could the sessions be improved?

4. What is on your mind that you wish you could say in the group?

4. Evaluation of Sessions

This evaluation form provides you with an opportunity to provide us with feedback about your experience of this program. Thank you very much for your time.

		Not Helpful at all					**Very Helpful**
1.	Generally, the sessions were:	0	1	2	3	4	5
2.	The session on assertiveness was:	0	1	2	3	4	5
3.	The session on goal-setting was:	0	1	2	3	4	5
4.	The session on problem-solving was:	0	1	2	3	4	5
5.	The session on self-esteem was:	0	1	2	3	4	5
6.	List of other topics:						
	_____	0	1	2	3	4	5
	_____	0	1	2	3	4	5
	_____	0	1	2	3	4	5
	_____	0	1	2	3	4	5
	_____	0	1	2	3	4	5
7.	The coach's facilitation of the group was:	0	1	2	3	4	5
8.	Overall, I found the experience in this group to be:	0	1	2	3	4	5

Additional Comments:

5. Lesson Evaluation

Please circle responses:

1. How was the organization of the lesson?

    (facilitator row images)

Excellent!   **Pretty Good**   **Needs a little work**   **Not so hot**   **Should be canned!**

2. How effective was the facilitator?

Excellent!   **Pretty Good**   **Needs a little work**   **Not so hot**   **Should be canned!**

3. The materials and ideas presented were:

Excellent!   **Pretty Good**   **Needs a little work**   **Not so hot**   **Should be canned!**

4. Overall, I consider this lesson:

Excellent!   **Pretty Good**   **Needs a little work**   **Not so hot**   **Should be canned!**

5. What are one or two things you particularly liked?

6. What do you think could have been done better today?

7. How do you think you will use what you have learned in this lesson?

8. Any other comments?

6. Group Behaviour Inventory

Name: Date:

Circle where you see yourself on the following scales:

HOW WELL DO YOU...	LOW				HIGH
Volunteer to speak out in the group	1	2	3	4	5
Express point of view honestly	1	2	3	4	5
Listen actively to others in the group	1	2	3	4	5
Ask for opinions and expression of ideas from others	1	2	3	4	5
Ask for information and facts related to the discussion	1	2	3	4	5
Ask questions to clarify what others have said	1	2	3	4	5
Express your feelings in or to the group	1	2	3	4	5
Help the group accomplish a goal	1	2	3	4	5
Carry out responsibilities arranged by the group	1	2	3	4	5
Co-operate with other members of the group	1	2	3	4	5
Support other group members who need help	1	2	3	4	5
Accept constructive criticism from the group	1	2	3	4	5

HOW WELL DO OTHERS...					
Pay attention to what you have to say	1	2	3	4	5
Seek suggestions or information from you	1	2	3	4	5
Seek opinions or feelings from you	1	2	3	4	5
Show they accept you as a group member	1	2	3	4	5
Support you when you need help	1	2	3	4	5

7. Group Evaluation Form

I Individual Effectiveness

1. My degree of involvement in the group was
   (a) high   (b) fairly high   (c) moderate   (d) low

2. My degree of influence on other group members was
   (a) high   (b) fairly high   (c) moderate   (d) low

3. My degree of commitment to accomplish group goals was
   (a) high   (b) fairly high   (c) moderate   (d) low

4. My degree of commitment to work on important group process issues was
   (a) high   (b) fairly high   (c) moderate   (d) low

II Group Effectiveness

1. The clarity of the task was
   (a) high   (b) fairly high   (c) moderate   (d) low

2. The leadership roles and function were
   (a) shared by all   (b) shared by most   (c) dominated by a few   (d) dominated by one

3. Important issues were handled
   (a) effectively   (b) fairly well   (c) adequately   (d) poorly

4. Communication channels were
   (a) open   (b) fairly open   (c) somewhat closed   (d) closed

5. The degree of acceptance of diverse viewpoints was
   (a) high   (b) fairly high   (c) moderate   (d) low

6. The climate of the group could be described as
   (a) trusting   (b) fairly trusting   (c) somewhat hostile   (d) hostile

7. The productivity of the group could be described as
   (a) high   (b) fairly high   (c) moderate   (d) low

8. Co-operation and teamwork were
   (a) evident   (b) fairly evident   (c) somewhat lacking (d) lacking

9. The degree of constructive problem-solving was
   (a) high   (b) fairly high   (c) moderate   (d) low

III Coach Effectiveness

1. The degree of enthusiasm was
   (a) high   (b) fairly high   (c) moderate   (d) low

2. The degree of effectiveness was
   (a) high   (b) fairly high   (c) moderate   (d) low

3. The coach's feedback was
   (a) descriptive   (b) fairly descriptive   (c) somewhat judgemental   (d) judgemental

   (a) specific   (b) fairly specific   (c) somewhat vague   (d) vague

   (a) constructive   (b) fairly constructive   (c) somewhat destructive   (d) destructive

   (a) well timed   (b) fairly well timed   (c) somewhat poorly timed   (d) poorly timed

IV Overall Effectiveness

1. The degree to which I was heard
   (a) high   (b) fairly high   (c) moderate   (d) low

2. The degree to which I listened was
   (a) high   (b) fairly high   (c) moderate   (d) low

3. The probability of applying others' input and ideas outside of the group is
   (a) high   (b) fairly high   (c) moderate   (d) low

4. The relevance of this experience to my current needs is
   (a) high   (b) fairly high   (c) moderate   (d) low

5. The relevance of this experience to my future needs is likely to be

(a) high   (b) fairly high   (c) moderate   (d) low

6. The probability that I will use the ideas acquired from this experience is likely to be
   (a) high   (b) fairly high   (c) moderate   (d) low

7. The probability that I will use the skills acquired from this experience is likely to be
   (a) high   (b) fairly high   (c) moderate   (d) low

Please provide comments or suggestions on areas not covered on this form. Indicate if they apply to you only, the group and/or the coach. Be as specific as possible. Thank you.

8. General Evaluation Survey

Name: Date:

Please circle your choice:	Low		Average		High

CONTENT:

1. The extent to which I understood the information presented was...

	1	2	3	4	5

2. The extent to which I agreed with the information presented was...

	1	2	3	4	5

3. The extent to which I valued the information presented was...

	1	2	3	4	5

PROCESS:

4. The degree to which the training met the needs of the group was...

	1	2	3	4	5

5. The degree of openness exhibited by the group was...

	1	2	3	4	5

6. The degree of spontaneity, humour and energy exhibited by the coach was...

	1	2	3	4	5

7. The degree to which the coach encouraged group cohesiveness, trust and responsiveness was...

	1	2	3	4	5

EXPERIENCE:

8. The amount of learning I experienced in this training was...

	1	2	3	4	5

9. The extent to which I enjoyed this training was...

	1	2	3	4	5

10. The extent to which this training
    was relevant to my goals was...   1   2   3   4   5

IMPACT:
11. Please list the experience(s) and/or information that held the greatest
    significance for you:

12. Please list the experience(s) and/or information that held the least
    significance for you:

13. How will you apply what you have learned in this training?

OTHER COMMENTS:

9. Evaluation: One Thing

1. One thing that stood out most in this course was:

2. One thing I learned about myself was:

3. One thing I feel I am improving as a result of this course is:

4. One thing I regret not having learned more about is:

5. One thing I wish had been done differently is:

6. One thing I'd still like to learn about after the course is:

10. Evaluation: A Snapshot

1. How do you feel about the program in general?

2. What was the most useful part of this program?

3. What was the least useful part? Why?

4. What have you learned that you can use in your home/work/school life?

5. What would you like to learn more about?

11. Lesson Evaluation Form

Title of Program: Date:

We would appreciate your feedback on the lesson. Please help us by filling out this evaluation form using the scale below. Please circle the appropriate value to answer the following:

1	2	3	4	5
Not at all satisfied		Somewhat satisfied		Very satisfied

1. To what extent were you satisfied:
    (a) that the goals were clearly identified at the beginning of the lesson?

        1   2   3   4   5

    (b) that the subject matter of the lesson met those goals?

        1   2   3   4   5

    (c) that the subject matter of the lesson was generally geared to your level of knowledge and experience?

        1   2   3   4   5

    (d) that you were encouraged to participate in and contribute to the lesson?

        1   2   3   4   5

    (e) that you will be able to use/apply the knowledge gained from the lesson?

        1   2   3   4   5

    (f) with the instructional methods used to present the subject matter?

        1   2   3   4   5

(g) that audiovisual aids were used effectively (if applicable)

1   2   3   4   5

(h) that the hand-out materials were useful? (if applicable)

1   2   3   4   5

(i) with the coach's level of expertise in the subject matter?

1   2   3   4   5

(j) with the coach's style of facilitation?

1   2   3   4   5

(k) that the lesson met your expectations?

1   2   3   4   5

2. As a result of this lesson, identify three new pieces of knowledge you have acquired:

3. What changes would you recommend to improve this session?

4. How will you use what you have learned today?

5. What further information would you like about this topic?

6. To improve the administrative aspects of our lessons we would appreciate your rating of the following. Please use the following rating scale:

	Not satisfied at all		Somewhat satisfied		Very satisfied
Location	1	2	3	4	5
Facilities	1	2	3	4	5
Length of Session	1	2	3	4	5

Other aspects/comments:

7. Overall comments:

Thanks!

12. How I See Myself Now

Name: Date:

Place an "X" on each line somewhere between 1 and 10 (1 = Never; 10 = Always):

I am a good listener
In group   1 _____ 10

Outside group   1 _____ 10

I understand what others are saying
In group   1 _____ 10

Outside group   1 _____ 10

I can express myself clearly
In group   1 _____ 10

Outside group   1 _____ 10

I am able to speak up in a group
In group   1 _____ 10

Outside group   1 _____ 10

I am assertive
In group   1 _____ 10

Outside group   1 _____ 10

I am aware of my feelings
In group   1 _____ 10

Outside group   1 _____ 10

I am aware of other people's feelings

In group   1 _____ 10

Outside group   1 _____ 10

I am able to say how I am feeling

In group   1 _____ 10

Outside group   1 _____ 10

I am able to make friends

In group   1 _____ 10

Outside group   1 _____ 10

I can challenge other people when I do not agree

In group   1 _____ 10

Outside group   1 _____ 10

I can confront other people when they are off topic or talking too much

In group   1 _____ 10

Outside group   1 _____ 10

I can express my views honestly

In group   1 _____ 10

Outside group   1 _____ 10

Skills I would like to work on in this group are:

13. Checklist for the Coach

The purpose of the checklist is to help the coach perform a self evaluation.

PRESENTATION
- Did I make the goals known at the beginning?
- Did I secure the attention and interest of the group members?
- Did I express ideas clearly?
- Did I motivate the group?
- Did I use communication aids effectively?
- Did I establish rapport with the group?
- Did I encourage participation?
- Did I use simple, understandable language?
- Did I use good questioning techniques?
- Did I make the best use of the available time?
- Did I use a variety of teaching methods?
- Did I summarize?
- Did I help establish a safe climate in the group?

MATERIAL
- Were materials appropriate for the group?
- Was it well organized?
- Did I explain and emphasize the main points?
- Were communication aids appropriate?
- Were handouts adequate?
- Were the case studies or examples relevant?

FACILITIES
- Was the physical environment satisfactory?
- Was the set-up of the room conducive to learning?

POST-COURSE
- Were the goals achieved? To what degree? If not, why not?
- Were the learner's goals met? How was this measured?
- What were the indications of change in knowledge, skills or attitudes?
- What methods worked well? Why?
- Which methods were not successful? Why?
- What improvements can be made in the material?
- Did I keep adequate records?

Bibliography: Historical

Curriculum Guide: Basic Life Skills. Alberta: Alberta NewStart, 1970.

Discovering Life Skills. Vol. 1-7. Toronto: YWCA of Metropolitan Toronto, 1976-1995.

Evaluations of Life Skills Training. Prince Albert, Saskatchewan: Saskatchewan NewStart, 1974.

Life Skills: A Course in Applied Problem Solving. Prince Albert Saskatchewan: Saskatchewan NewStart, 1973.

Life Skills Coach Training Manual. Prince Albert Saskatchewan: Saskatchewan NewStart, 1971.

Life Skills Coaching Manual. Prince Albert, Saskatchewan: Saskatchewan NewStart, 1973.

Life Skills Course for Corrections. Prince Albert, Saskatchewan: Saskatchewan NewStart, n.d.

Life Skills Curriculum: Trainee Guide and Instructor Guide. Prince Albert, Saskatchewan: Saskatchewan NewStart, 1969.

Life Skills for Northern Adolescents. Prince Albert, Saskatchewan: Saskatchewan NewStart and Training Research and Development Station, 1970.

Life Skills Research Endeavours. Prince Albert, Saskatchewan: Saskatchewan NewStart. 1970.

Life Skills: Social Process Exercises. St. Paul, Minnesota: Instructional Simulations, 1972.

Methods for Human Resource Development. Prince Albert Saskatchewan: Training Research and Development Station, 1973.

Moving on! (series). Ottawa: Occupational and Career Analysis and Development Branch, Advanced Development Division, Employment and Immigration Canada, 1980.

Place: Guided Steps to Employment Readiness. Ottawa: Occupational and Career Analysis and Development Branch, Employment and Immigration Canada, 1980.

Readings in Life Skills. Prince Albert, Saskatchewan: Saskatchewan NewStart and Training Research and Development Station, 1973.

Saskatchewan NewStart Life Skills Curriculum: Trainee Guide and Instructor Guide. Prince Albert, Saskatchewan: Saskatchewan NewStart, 1970.

Socanic Coaching Manual. Prince Albert, Saskatchewan: Saskatchewan NewStart, 1972.

The Dynamics of Life Skills Coaching. Prince Albert, Saskatchewan: Training Research and Development Station, Department of Manpower and Immigration, 1973.

The Problems and Needed Life Skills of Adolescents. Prince Albert: Saskatchewan NewStart and Training Research and Development Station, 1972.

Training the Life Skills Coach. Prince Albert, Saskatchewan: Saskatchewan NewStart and Training Research and Development Station, (series of publications), 1970-1974.

Adkins, Winthrop. Life Coping Skills: A Fifth Curriculum, in *Teachers College Record.* Vol. 75, 1974.

Adkins, Winthrop. Life Skills for Adult Learners. *Adult Leadership.* Vol. 22, No. 2, June, 1973.

Adkins, Winthrop et al. One Institution: Six Alternatives. *Junior College Review.* Vol. 5, No. 9, May 1971.

Adkins, Winthrop and Sidney Rosenberg. *A Design for Action Research at Project TRY: Final Report.* Brooklyn, N.Y.: Training Resources for Youth Inc., 1965.

Adkins, Winthrop and Sidney Rosenberg. *TRY: Training Resources for Youth.* Brooklyn, N.Y.: Training Resources for Youth, Inc., 1965.

Adkins, Winthrop and Sidney Rosenberg. *Report of Research Design and Information System Task Force.* Prince Albert, Saskatchewan: Saskatchewan NewStart, 1968.

Adkins, Winthrop. Life Skills: Structured Counselling for the Disadvantaged, *Personnel and Guidance Journal.* Vol. 49, No. 2 , 1970.

Adkins, Winthrop et al. *Where They Hurt: A Study of Life Coping Problems of Unemployed Adults.* New York: Unpublished Manuscript, Teachers College, Columbia University, 1977.

Adkins Winthrop et al. *Adkins Life Skills Program: Employability Skills Series.* New York: The Psychological Corporation, 1975.

Bandura, Albert. *Principle of Behaviour Modification.* Florida: Holt, Rinehart and Winston, 1969.

Bandura, Albert. *Social Learning and Personality Development.* Florida: Holt, Rinehart and Winston, 1963.

Bandura, Albert. *Social Learning Theory.* New Jersey: Prentice Hall, 1977.

Bandura, Albert. Self-efficacy Mechanism in Human Agency. *American Psychologist,* no. 37, 1982.

Bennis, Warren et al. *The Planning of Change.* Florida: Holt, Rinehart and Winston, 1962.

Berne, Eric. *Transactional Analysis in Psychotherapy.* New York: Grove Press, 1961.

Brundage, Donald and Dorothy MacKeracher. *Adult Learning Principles and Their Application to Program Planning.* Ontario: Ministry of Education, 1980.

Carkhuff, R. *The Art of Helping - An Introduction to Life Skills.* Amherst, Mass.: HRD, 1973.

Carkhuff, R. *The Art of Problem Solving.* Amherst, Mass.: HRD, 1973.

Conger, Stuart. Developing Social and Life Skills, Commentary on the British Report. *Developing Social and Life Skills.* Ottawa: Occupational and Career Analysis and Development Branch, Advanced Development Division, Employment and Immigration Canada, April, 1980.

Conger, Stuart. *Recent Developments in Life Skills Training.* Talk given at the Life Skills Coach Conference, Toronto, April 26, 1979.

Conger, Stuart. Saskatchewan NewStart. *Canadian Vocational Journal*, Vol. 6, No. 3, May 1970.

Crawford, R. *The Techniques of Creative Thinking: How to Use Your Ideas to Achieve Success.* Burlington, Vermont: Fraser, 1954.

Cranton, Patricia A. *Planning Instruction for Adult Learners.* Toronto: Wall and Thompson, 1989.

Curtiss, Paul, and Phillip Warren. *The Dynamics of Life Skills Coaching.* Prince Albert, Saskatchewan: Saskatchewan NewStart, 1973.

Dale, Edgar. *Audio-Visual Methods in Teaching.* New York: Dryden, 1954.

Davidson, C. and G. Tippet. *A Career Planning Guide.* Prince Albert, Saskatchewan: Training, Research and Development Station, 1977.

Davidson, C., and G. Tippet. *Creating a Career and Job Workbook.* Prince Albert, Saskatchewan: Training, Research and Development Station, 1977.

Davidson, C., and G. Tippet. *Creating a Career: Instructors' Manual.* Prince Albert, Saskatchewan: Training, Research and Development Station, 1977.

Dimock, Hedley. *How to Analyze and Evaluate Group Growth.* Montreal: Concordia University, 1970.

Friedman, Ronald. *Training the Life Skills Coach.* Prince Albert, Saskatchewan: Saskatchewan NewStart, 1970.

Friere, Paulo. *Pedagogy of the Oppressed.* New York: Continuum, 1981.

Giroux, Roy et al. A Community Based Corrections Program in *Michigan Personnel and Guidance Journal.* Vol. 5, No. 2, 1974.

Giroux, Roy, et al. *Vocational Preparatory Program: An Evaluation of the Vocational Preparatory Program: A Summary.* Windsor, Ontario: St. Clair College, 1973.

Glasser, William. *Reality Therapy.* New York: Harper and Row, 1965.

Glover, Chris. *Investigating Life Skills.* Unpublished Paper, 1992.

Gryba, E., and R. Kyba. *A Plan For a Life Skills Course for Northern Adolescents.* Prince Albert, Saskatchewan: Saskatchewan NewStart, 1972.

Hamilton, G.W. *Nova Scotia NewStart Life Skills Programme.* Yarmouth, Nova Scotia: Nova Scotia NewStart, n.d.

Harris, Thomas. *I'm O.K., You're O.K.: A Practical Guide to Transactional Analysis.* New York: Harper, 1969.

Hearn, Joan. *More Life Skills.* Ottawa: Occupational and Career Analysis Development Branch, Advanced Development Division, Employment and Immigration Canada, 1981.

Herzog, A., and L. Denton. *Some Considerations for the Evaluation of NewStart Action-Research Programs.* Nova Scotia: Nova Scotia NewStart Inc., 1970.

Himsl, Ralph. Life Skills in Manpower Training, *Canadian Vocational Journal.* Vol. 6, No. 4, 1972.

Hodnett, E. *The Art of Problem-Solving: How to Improve your Methods.* New York: Harper and Row, 1995.

Hopson, B., and M. Scally. *Lifeskills Teaching Programmes.* Leeds, England: Lifeskills Associates, 1979.

Ivey, Allen. *Microcounselling.* Springfield, Illinois: Charles C. Thomas, 1971.

Kirpatrick, Donald. Techniques for Evaluating Training Programs. *Training and Development Journal.* Wisconsin, 1978.

Knowles, Malcolm. *Introduction to Group Dynamics.* New York: Association Press, 1972.

Knowles, Malcolm. *Self-Directed Learning: A Guide for Learners and Teachers.* Chicago: Association, 1975.

Knowles, Malcolm. *The Modern Practise of Adult Education: From Pedagogy to Andragogy.* New Jersey: Prentice Hall, 1980.

Kolb, David. *Experiental Learning: Experience as the Source of Learning and Development.* New Jersey: Prentice Hall, 1974.

Kramarae, Cheris and Paula Treichler. *A Feminist Dictionary.* London: Pandora, 1990.

Lamrock, L. *Demographic Information, Intakes A,B,C,D,and E.* Prince Albert, Saskatchewan: Saskatchewan NewStart, 1970.

Lamrock, L. et al. *Evaluation: Its Scope and Systems for Evaluation Development.* Paper presented at the meeting of Research Directors of NewStart Corporations. Ottawa, 1971.

Lavender, Matti. *Life Skills Manual for Upgrading Students.* Oakville, Ontario: Sheridan College, 1975.

Levan, Mary Beth. *Lodestar: Life Skills Coach Training Manual.* North West Territories: Native Women's Association, 1986.

Maslow, Abraham. *Toward a Psychology of Being.* New York: Van Nostrand, 1968.

May, Rolo. *Love and Will.* London: Souvenir, 1970.

Mehal, Mickey. *Life Skills: Some Recent Developments.* Toronto: Unpublished Manuscript, Department of Adult Education, Ontario Institute for Studies in Education, University of Toronto, 1981.

Mullen, Dana. *A Conceptual Framework for the Life Skills Program.* Ottawa: Occupational and Career Analysis and Development Branch, Advanced Development Division, Employment and Immigration Canada, 1981.

Parnes, Sidney. *Creative Behaviour Guidebook.* Baltimore: Charles Scribner, 1967.

Perles, Fritz. *Gestalt Therapy Verbatim.* Lafayette, California: Real People, 1969.

Rogers, Carl. *Client-Centered Therapy.* Boston: Houghton Mifflin, 1951.

Rogers, Carl. *On Becoming a Person.* Boston: Houghton Mifflin, 1961.

Rosove, Bruce. *Employment Assessment: Its Importance and One Way of Doing It.* Ottawa: Occupational and Career Analysis and Development Branch, Employment and Immigration Canada, 1981.

Rubin, L., ed. *Life Skills in School and Society.* Washington: Association for Supervision and Curriculum Development, 1969.

Sellon Larry et al. Synectics and Fantasy: Their Use in a Life Skills Program, *Training 75/Formation 75.* Vol. 1, No. 1, 1975.

Sellon, Larry. *The Effects of Life Skills Training on Attitudes, Values and Self Concept.* Unpublished paper, 1975.

Shostrom, Everett. *Man The Manipulator: The Inner Journey From Manipulation to Actualization.* New York: Bantam, 1967.

Sloan, E.P. The Canada NewStart Program: An Overview. *Coming of Age: Canadian Adult Education in the 1960's.* Edited by J. Roby Kidd and Gordon Selman. Toronto: Canadian Association for Adult Education, 1978.

Skinner, B.F. *The Technology of Teaching.* Appleton-Century-Crofts, 1968.

Smith, Arthur. *Generic Skills: Keys to Job Performance.* Ottawa: Occupational and Career Analysis Development Branch, Advanced Development Division, Employment and Immigration Canada, 1978.

Smith, Arthur et al. *A Systematic and Behavioural Approach to Counselling.* Ottawa: Occupational and Career Analysis and Development Branch, Advanced Development Division, Employment and Immigration Canada, 1975.

Smith, Manuel. *When I Say No, I Feel Guilty: How to Cope--Using the Skills of Systematic Assertive Therapy.* New York: Dial, 1975.

Smith, Paul. *The Development of a Taxonomy of the Life Skills to Become a Balanced Self-Determined Person.* Ottawa: Occupational and Career Analysis Development Branch, Employment and Immigration Canada, 1981.

Smith, Paul and Debbie White. *Life Skills Coach Training Program.* Ontario: Training Improvement Project (TIP), report #7874, Ministry of Colleges and Universities, 1979.

Stanton, G.P. et al. *Developing Social and Life Skills: Strategies for Tutors.* London, England: Further Education Curriculum Review and Development Unit, 1980.

Tough, Allen. *The Adult's Learning Projects: A Fresh Approach to Theory and Practise in Adult Learning.* Toronto: Ontario Institute for Studies in Education, 1971.

Tuckman, Bruce. Development Sequence in Small Group. *Psychological Bulletin.* No. 63 (6), 1965.

Waite, N. *Case Studies and the Case Method.* Prince Albert, Saskatchewan: Saskatchewan NewStart, 1970.

Warren, Phillip., ed. *Principles of "Behaviour Modification", "Contingency Contracting" and "Skill Training".* Prince Albert, Saskatchewan: Saskatchewan NewStart, 1972.

Warren, Phillip et al. *Interim Report of Evaluation System and Procedures.* Prince Albert, Saskatchewan: Saskatchewan NewStart, 1971.

Warren, Phillip et al. *Effects of the Life Skills Course on Personality and Attitude Measures: A Preliminary Report.* Prince Albert, Saskatchewan: Saskatchewan NewStart (n.d.)

Warren, Phillip and A. Lamrock. Evaluation of the Life Skills Course, *Life Skills: A Course in Applied Problem Solving.* Prince Albert, Saskatchewan: Saskatchewan NewStart, 1972.

Warren, Phillip. *The Problems and Needed Life Skills of Adolescents.* Prince Albert, Saskatchewan: Saskatchewan NewStart, 1969.

Warren, Phillip. *The Role of Research in Research and Development Programs.* Prince Albert, Saskatchewan: Saskatchewan NewStart, 1969.

Watkinson, Susan. *Life Skills Coaching Manual: A Continuous Intake Dacum Approach.* Stratford, Ontario: Training Associates, 1976.

Williams, J. and E. Mardell. *Life Skills Course for Corrections.* Prince Albert, Saskatchewan: Saskatchewan NewStart for Training Research and Development Station, 1973.

Wilson, John et al. *Introduction to Moral Education.* Baltimore: Penguin, 1967.

Zelner A. *Life Skills: Female Images.* St. Paul, Minnesota: Instructional Simulations, 1972.

Zenger, John. A Comparison of Human Development with Psychological Development in Training Groups. *Training and Development Journal,* 1970.

Bibliography: Process

Adler, Ronald et al. *Interplay.* Florida: Holt, Rinehart and Winston, 1983.

Adler Ronald and Neil Towne. *Looking Out/Looking In:Interpersonal Communication.* New York: Holt Rinehart, 1993.

Adler, Ronald and George Rodman. *Understanding Human Communication.* Florida: Holt, Rinehart and Winston, 1991.

Albrecht, Lisa and Rose Brewer (ed). *Bridges of Power: Women's Multicultural Alliances.* Philadelphia: New Society, 1990.

Barker B. et al. *Groups in Process.* Boston: Allyn and Bacon, 1995.

Benjamin, Alfred. *Behaviour In Small Groups.* Boston: Houghton Mifflin, 1988.

Beebe, Steven and John Masterson. *Communicating in Small Groups: Principles and Practices. Illinois: Harper Collins, 1994.*

Belenky, Mary Field et. al. Women's Ways of Knowing. New York: Basic, 1986.

Berko, Roy et al. *Communicating.* Boston: Houghton Mifflin, 1992.

Berko, Roy et al. *Connecting: A Culture-Sensitive Approach to Interpersonal Communication Competency and Instructors' Manual.* Florida: Harcourt Brace, 1994.

Bilken, Douglas. *Community Organizing.* New Jersey: Prentice Hall, 1983.

Bormann, Ernest. *Small Group Communication.* Michigan: Harper and Row, 1990.

Bradford, Leland, ed. *Group Development.* California: University Associates, 1978.

Bramner, Lawrence. *The Helping Relationship.* New Jersey: Prentice Hall, 1988.

Chiaramonte, Peter and Marco Adria. *Face-to-Face: Interpersonal Communication in the Workplace.* Scarborough, Ontario: Prentice Hall, 1994.

Cohen, Arthur and Douglas Smith. *Critical Incidents in Group.* California: University Associates, 1974.

Cole, J. *Filtering People: Understanding and Confronting Our Prejudices.* Pennsylvania: New Society, 1990.

Corey, Gerald and Marianne Corey. *A Casebook of Ethical Guidelines For Group Leaders.* California: Brooks/Cole, 1982.

Corey, Gerald. *Theory and Practise of Group Counselling.* California: Brooks/Cole, 1995.

Corey, Gerald and Marianne Corey. *Groups: Process and Practise.* California: Brooks/Cole, 1992.

Corey, Gerald and Marianne Corey. *Group Techniques.* California: Brooks/Cole, 1992.

Cormier, L. Sherilyn and Harold Hackney. *The Professional Counsellor: A Process Guide to Helping.* New Jersey: Prentice Hall, 1987.

Cragan, John and David Wright. *Communication in Small Group Discussions: An Integrated Approach.* Minnesota: West, 1995.

Devito, Joseph. *The Interpersonal Communication Book.* New York: Harper Collins, 1995.

Devito, Joseph. *Messages.* New York: Harper Collins, 1992.

Dimock, Hedley. *Groups: Leadership and Group Development.* California: University Associates, 1987.

Dimock, Hedley. *How to Observe Your Group.* Guelph: University of Guelph, 1985.

Donigian, Jeremiah and Richard Malnati. *Critical Incidents in Group Therapy.* California: Brooks/Cole, 1987.

Eberhardt, Louise Yolton. *Working With Women's Groups, Volumes I and II.* Duluth Minnesota: Whole Person, 1987.

Egan, Gerard. *Face To Face.* California: Brooks/Cole, 1973.

Egan, Gerard. *You And Me.* California: Brooks/Cole, 1977.

Ellis, Donald and B. Aubrey Fisher. *Small Group Decision Making: Communication and the Group Process.* New York: McGraw-Hill, 1994.

Eriksen, Karin. *Communication Skills For The Human Services.* New Jersey: Prentice Hall, 1979.

Gadza, George. *Group Counselling.* Boston: Allyn and Bacon, 1984.

Garvin, George. *Contemporary Group Work.* New Jersey: Prentice Hall, 1987.

Gastil, John. *Democracy in Small Groups.* Philadelphia: New Society, 1993.

George, Rickey and Therese Cristiani. *Counselling, Theory, and Practice.* New Jersey: Prentice Hall, 1986.

George, Rickey and Dick Dustin. *Group Counselling, Theory and Practice.* New Jersey: Prentice Hall, 1988.

Gladding, Samuel. *Group Work: A Counselling Specialty.* New York: Macmillan, 1991.

Glaser, Susan and Anna Eblen. *Toward Communication Competency.* New York: Holt, Rinehart, and Winston, 1986.

Gudykunst, William, and Young Yu Kim. *Communicating With Strangers: An Approach To Intercultural Communication.* New York: McGraw-Hill, 1992.

Hackney, Harold, and Sherilyn L. Cormier. *Counselling, Strategies and Intervention.* Boston: Allyn and Bacon, 1994.

Hamachek, Don. *Encounters With Others.* New York: Holt Rinehart and Winston, 1982.

Hart, Lois. *Faultless Facilitation: An Instructor's Manual for Facilitation Training.* Massachusettes: HRD, 1992.

Hart, Lois. *Training Methods that Work: A Handbook for Trainers.* California: Crisp, 1991.

Hobson, Barrie, and Mike Scalley. *Communication: Skills to Inspire Confidence.* California: Pfeiffer, 1993.

hooks, bell. *Feminist Theory: from Margin to Center.* Boston: South End, 1984.

Ivey, Allen et al. *Counselling and Psychotherapy.* New Jersey: Prentice Hall, 1987.

Jacobs, Ed et al. *Group Counselling: Strategies and Skills.* California: Brooks/Cole, 1994.

James, Carl. *Seeing Ourselves: Exploring Race, Ethnicity and Culture.* Toronto: Thompson, 1995.

Johnson, David. *Reaching Out: Interpersonal Effectiveness and Self-Actualization.* New Jersey: Prentice Hall, 1993.

Johnson, David and Frank Johnson. *Joining Together.* New Jersey: Prentice Hall, 1994.

Karsk, Roger, and Bill Thomas. *Working With Men's Groups.* Duluth: Whole Person, 1987.

Keleman, K. *Jumpstarting Your New Team: Establishing Norms.* California: Pfeiffer, 1994.

Kindler, H. *Managing Disagreement Constructively: Conflict Management in Organizations.* California: Crisp, 1988.

Kokopeli, B., and G. Lakey. *Leadership for Change: Toward a Feminist Model.* Pennsylvania: n.d.

Konopka, Gisela. *Social Group Work.* New Jersey: Prentice Hall, 1983.

Knapp, Mark, and Judith Hall. *Nonverbal Communication In Human Interaction.* Florida: Holt Rinehart and Winston, 1992.

LaMountain, Dianne, and Bob Abramms. *The Trainer's Workshop on Cultural Diversity.* Massachusettes: HRD, 1993.

Lassey, W.R. and M. Sashkin, eds. *Leadership and Social Change.* California: University Associates, 1983.

Lee, Courtland. *Counselling for Diversity.* Boston: Allyn and Bacon, 1995.

Leigh, David. *A Practical Approach to Group Training.* California: Pfeiffer, 1991.

Lightle, J. and B. Doucet. *Sexual Harassment in the Workplace: A Guide to Prevention.* California: Crisp, 1992.

Lumsden Donald and Gay Lumsden. *Communicating in Groups and Teams.* California: Wadsworth, 1993.

Lustig, Myron and Jolene Koester. *Intercultural Competence.* Harper Collins, 1993.

MacKinnon, Catharine. *Feminism Unmodified.* New York: Howard, 1987.

Margulies, S., and C.E. Crowell. *Readings in Cultural Literacy: Topics Across the Curriculum.* New York: Educational Design, 1991.

McGrath, Joseph. *Groups, Interaction and Performance.* New Jersey: Prentice Hall, 1984.

Millet, Kate. *Sexual Politics.* New York: Doubleday, 1976.

Minor, M. *Coaching and Counselling: A Practical Guide for Managers.* California: Crisp, 1989.

Morgan, Robin (ed). *Sisterhood is Global.* New York: Anchor, 1994.

Napier, Rodney, and Mikki Gershenfeld. *Groups: Theory and Experience.* Boston: Houghton Mifflin, 1993.

Nelson-Jones, Richard. *Group Leadership: A Training Approach.* California: Brooks/Cole, 1992.

Nelson-Jones, Richard. *Lifeskills Helping.* California: Brooks/Cole, 1993.

Olmstead, Michael. *The Small Group.* New York: Random House, 1959.

Pollar, O. and R. Gonzalez. *Dynamics of Diversity: Strategic Programs for Your Organization.* California: Crisp, 1994.

Reddy, W. Brendan. *Intervention Skills: Process Consultation for Small Groups and Teams.* California: Pfeiffer, 1994.

Rees, Fran. *How to Lead Work Teams: Facilitation Skills.* California: Pfeiffer and Company, 1991.

Rogers, Carl. *On Encounter Groups.* New York: Harper Collins, 1970.

Ross, Raymond. *Small Groups in Organizational Settings.* New Jersey: Prentice Hall, 1989.

Rothwell, J. Dan. *In Mixed Company.* Fort Worth: Holt Rinehart and Winston, 1992.

Rudeston, Kjell. *Experiential Groups: In Theory and Practice.* California: Brooks/Cole, 1982.

Schmuck, Richard and Patricia Schmuck. *Group Processes In The Classroom.* New York: William Brown, 1975.

Shaw, Marvin. *Group Dynamics: The Psychology of Small Group Behaviour.* New York: McGraw-Hill, 1976.

Steinem, Gloria. *Revolution from Within.* New York: Little Brown, 1990.

Sue, Derald Wing and David Sue. *Counselling the Culturally Different: Theory and Practise.* New York: John Wiley, 1990.

Thomas, Barb. *Multiculturalism at Work: A Guide to Organizational Change.* Toronto: YWCA of Metropolitan Toronto, 1987.

Toseland, Ronald and Robert Rivas. *An Introduction to Group Work Practise.* Boston: Allyn and Bacon, 1995.

Tubbs, Stewart. *A Systems Approach to Small Group Interaction.* New York: McGraw-Hill, 1992.

Verderber, Rudolph and Kathleen Verderber. *Interact: Using Interpersonal Skills.* California: Wadsworth, 1995.

Verderber, Kathleen. *Voices: A Selection of Multicultural Readings.* California: Wadsworth, 1995.

Walker, Barbara. *The Skeptical Feminist: Discovering Virgin Mother and Crone.* San Francisco: Harper and Row, 1987.

Weaver, Richard. *Understanding Interpersonal Communication.* New York: Harper Collins, 1993.

Wheelan, Susan. *Group Processes: A Developmental Perspective.* Boston: Allyn and Bacon, 1994.

Wickham, Edcil. *Group Treatment in Social Work: An Integration of Theory and Practice.* Toronto: Thompson, 1992.

Wilson, Gerald and Michael Hanna. *Groups in Context: Leadership and Participation in Small Groups.* New York: McGraw-Hill, 1993.

Woodrow, P. *Clearness: Processes for Supporting Individuals and Groups in Decision Making.* Pennsylvania: New Society, 1976.

Bibliography: Activities

Adilman, Audrey et al. *Core Lessons for Life Skills Programs.* British Columbia: Province of British Columbia, Ministry of Skills Training and Labour and the Centre for Curriculum and Professional Development, 1994.

Advancement Strategies. *Diversity Bingo: An Experiential Learning Event.* California: Pfeiffer, 1992.

Amundson, Norman et al. *Group Employment Counselling: Theory and Techniques.* Ottawa: Canada Employment and Immigration.

Avery, M. et al. *Building United Judgement: A Handbook for Consensus Decision Making.* Wisconsin: The Center For Conflict Resolution, 1981.

Bargo, Michael. *Choices and Decisions: A Guidebook for Constructing Values.* California: University Associates, 1980.

Bargo, Michael. *A Facilitator's Manual for: Choices and Decisions.* California: University Associates, 1980.

Bass, G. et al. *Nuclear Site Negotiation.* California: University Associates, 1982.

Bianchi, Sue et al. *Warmups For Meeting Leaders.* California: University Associates, 1990.

Bolles, Richard. *What Color Is Your Parachute.* California: Ten Speed, 1995.

Bower, Sharon, and Gordon Bower. *Asserting Yourself: A Practical Guide For Positive Change.* Massachusetts: Addison-Wesley, 1991.

Bozek, P.E. *50 One-Minute Tips for Better Communication.* California: Crisp, 1991.

Branden, Nathaniel. *A Guide To Self Discovery.* New York: Bantam, 1989.

Branden, Nathaniel. *How To Raise Your Self Esteem.* New York: Bantam, 1988.

Breen, Mary. *Taking Care: A Handbook About Women's Health.* Thorn, 1988.

Brewner, M.M. et al. *Job Survival Skills.* New York: Educational Design, 1993.

Brewner, M.M. et al. *Life Skills Attitudes in Everyday Living.* New York: Educational Design, 1991.

Brody, E. et al. *Spinning Tales, Weaving Hope: Stories of Peace Justice and the Environment.* British Columbia: New Society, 1992.

Butler, Pamela. *Self-Assertion For Women.* California: Harper and Row, 1981.

Canfield, Jack and Harold Wells. *One Hundred Ways To Enhance Self-Concept In The Classroom.* New Jersey: Prentice Hall, 1976.

Carse, James. *Finite and Infinite Games: A Vision of Life and Play and Possibility.* New York: MacMillan, 1986.

Chapman, Elwood. *I Got The Job: Win a Job Your Way.* California: Crisp, 1988.

Christopher, L. et al. *Experiential Workshops for Teachers: A Facilitators Manual.* North Carolina: Charlotte Drug Education Center, 1979.

Church, Olive, and Delores Gade. *Interpersonal Communication: 50 Copy Masters.* Maine: J. Weston Walch, 1979.

Cibiri, Stephen, and Lloyd Jackson. *Training Developmentally Handicapped Persons: Basic Life Skills - a Task Analysis Approach.* Toronto: Ministry of Community and Social Services, 1981.

Cinnamon, Kenneth and Norman Matulef. *Human Relations Development.* California: Applied Skills, 1979.

Coovep, V. et al. *Resource Manual for a Living Revolution: A Handbook of Skills and Tools for Social Change Activists.* British Columbia: New Society, 1985.

Cox, Geof, et al. *50 Activities For Creativity and Problem Solving.* Massachusetts: HRD, 1991.

Christopher, Linda et al., eds. *Experiential Workshops for Teachers: A Facilitator's Manual.* North Carolina: Charlotte Drug Education, 1979.

Dagget, William, and Martin Marrazo. *Solving Problems/Making Decisions.* Ohio: South Western, 1983.

Daniels, W.R. *Group Power I: A Manager's Guide to Using Task Force Meetings.* California: University, 1986.

Daniels, W.R. *Group Power II: A Manager's Guide to Using Regular Meetings.* California: University Associates, 1986.

De Bono, Edward. *Serious Creativity: Using the Power of Lateral Thinking to Create New Ideas.* New York: Harper Business, 1992.

Department of Education. *Coping Skills in a Changing Environment. Vol. 1 and 2.* Northwest Territories: n.d.

Discovering Life Skills, Vol. 1-7. Toronto: YWCA of Metropolitan Toronto, 1976-1995.

Donnan, Linda and Sue Lenton. *Helping Ourselves.* London, England: Women's, 1990.

Dossick, Jane and Eugene Shea. *Creative Therapy: 52 Exercises for Groups.* Professional Exchange, 1988.

Dossick, Jane and Eugene Shea. *Creative Therapy II: 52 More exercises for Groups.* Professional Exchange, 1990.

Egan, Gerard. *Exercises In Helping Skills.* California: Brooks/Cole, 1982.

Employment and Immigration Canada. *PLACE: Guided Steps To Employment Readiness.* Ottawa: Minister of Supply and Services, 1980.

Employment and Immigration Canada. *Moving On by Staying On.* Ottawa: Minister of Supply and Services, 1980.

Employment and Immigration Canada. *Tuning In: Intentional Attending.* Ottawa: Advanced Development Division, Occupation and Career Development Branch, 1980.

Filger, Sharon, ed. *Preparing For Change.* Toronto: Opportunity For Advancement, 1989.

Fisher, D. Joseph and D.M. Peters. *Earthquake: A Team Building Simulation.* Michigan: Orion, 1990.

Fisher, D. Joseph and D.M. Peters. *Earthquake: Facilitator's Guide.* Michigan: Orion, 1990.

Fox, William and Rollin Glaser. *Improved Nominal Group Technique: Participant Guide.* Pennsylvania: Organization Design and Development, 1990.

Fox, William and Rollin Glaser. *Improved Nominal Group Technique: Trainer Guide.* Pennsylvania: Organization Design and Development, 1990.

Forbes-Greene, Sue. *The Encyclopedia Of Icebreakers.* California: Applied Skills Press, 1989.

Forsey, H., ed. *Circles of Strength: Community Alternatives to Alienation.* British Columbia: New Society, 1993.

Gawain, Shakti. *Creative Visualization.* California: New World, 1978.

Gawain, Shakti. *Creative Visualization Workbook.* California: New World, 1982.

Gawain, Shakti. *Reflections in the Light: Daily Thoughts and Affirmations.* California: New World, 1988.

Gelatt, H.B. *Creative Decision-Making: Using Positive Uncertainty.* California: Crisp, 1991.

Glaser, Rollin. *The Force-Field Problem-Solving Model: Exercise.* Pennsylvania: Organization Design and Development, 1984.

Glaser, Rollin. *The Force-Field Problem-Solving Model: Trainer Guide.* Pennsylvania: Organization Design and Development, 1984.

Glaser, Rollin. *Silence Speaks Ouder Than Words: Nonverbal Sensitivity Training.* Pennsylvania: Organization Design and Development, 1983.

Goad, Tom. *Delivering Effective Training.* California: University Associates, 1982.

Green, Tova and Peter Woodrow. *Insight and Action: How to Discover and Support a Life of Integrity and Commitment to Change.* British Columbia: New Society, 1994.

Guthrie, Eileen et al. *Process Politics.* California: University Associates, 1981.

Hackett, D. and Martin, C.L. *Facilitation Skills for Team Leaders.* California: Crisp, 1993.

Hale, Ann. *Conducting Clinical Sociometric Explorations.* Roanoke Virginia., 1981.

Hall, Jay. *Conflict Management: Styles of Teamwork Inventory.* Texas: Teleometrics International, 1986.

Hall, Jay, *NASA Moon Survival Task: Team Process Diagnostic.* Texas: Teleometrics International, 1986.

Handbook for Life Skills Coaches. Edmonton, Alberta: Grant MacEwan College, n.d.

Harmin, Merill and Saville Sax. *A Peaceful Classroom: Activities To Calm and Free Student Energies.* Minnesota: Winston, 1977.

Harris, Brian. *A Self Awareness Workbook.* Toronto: Guidance Centre, University Of Toronto, 1982.

Hart, Lois. *Training Methods that Work: A Handbook for Trainers.* California: Crisp, 1991.

Hart, Lois. *Faultless Facilitation: A Resource Guide for Group and Team Leaders.* Massachusetts: HRD, 1992.

Hart, Lois. *Faultless Facilitation: A Handbook for Trainers.* Massachusetts: Crisp, 1992.

Harvey, Carol and M. June Allard. *Understanding Diversity: Readings, Cases and Exercises.* New York: Harper Collins, 1995.

Harvey, Carol and M. June Allard. *Instructor's Manual to Accompany Understanding Diversity.* New York: Harper Collins, 1995.

Heider, John. *The Tao of Leadership: Leadership Strategies for a New Age.* New York: Bantam, 1985.

Hendricks, Gay and Thomas Roberts. *The Second Centering Book.* Englewood Cliffs,New Jersey: Prentice Hall, 1977.

Hersey, Paul and Ken Blanchard. *Situational Leadership.* California: University Associates, 1976.

Hersey, Paul and Joseph Keilty. *Situation Leadership.* California: University Associates, 1980.

Hill, Richard et al. *Group Process: Questionnaire.* Michigan: Orion, 1988.

Hill, Richard et al. *Group Process: Facilitator's Guide.* Michigan: Orion, 1988.

Hopson, Barrie and Mike Scalley. *Assertiveness: A Positive Process.* California: Pfeiffer, 1993.

Hopson, Barrie and Mike Scalley. *Time Management: Conquering the Clock.* California: Pfeiffer, 1993.

Hopson, Barrie and Mike Scalley. *Transitions: Positive Change in Your Life and Work.* California: Pfeiffer, 1993.

Ivey, Allen and Norma Gluckstern. *Basic Attending Skills.* Massachusetts: Microtraining Association, 1974.

James, Muriel and Dorothy Jongeward. *Born To Win.* Massachusetts: Addison Wesley, 1973.

Jones, Ken. *Icebreakers.* California: Pfeiffer, 1991.

Judson, S., ed. *A Manual on Non-Violence and Children.* Pennsylvania: New Society, 1984.

Kelley, Colleen. *Assertion Training: A Facilitator's Guide.* California: University Associates, 1979.

Keleman, K.S. *Jumpstarting Your New Team: Establishing Norms.* California: Pfeiffer, 1994.

Kimeldorf, M. *Job Search Education.* New York: Educational Designs, 1988.

Kindler, H.S. *Managing Disagreement Constructively: Conflict Management in Organizations.* California: Crisp, 1988.

Kinlaw, Dennis. *Listening And Communications Skills.* California: University Associates, 1981.

Kirby, Andy. *The Encyclopedia Of Games For Trainers.* Maine: HRD Press, 1992.

Kirby, Andy, ed. *A Compendium of Icebreakers, Energizers and Introductions.* Massachusetts: HRD, 1992.

Knapp, Mark and Judith Hall. *Nonverbal Communication in Human Interaction.* Florida: Holt, Rinehart and Winston, 1992.

Krusell, Judith, et al. *Personal and Interpersonal Development: A Self-Administered Workbook.* California: University Associates, 1982.

LaMountain, Dianne and Bob Abrams. *The Trainers' Workshop on Cultural Diversity.* Massachusetts: HRD, 1993.

Lange, Arthur J. and Patricia Jakubowski. *Responsible Assertive Behavior.* Illinois: Research Press, 1976.

Leider, Richard. *Life Skills: Taking Charge of Your Personal and Professional Growth.* California, Pfeiffer, 1994.

Lirdenfield, Gael. *Assert Yourself: A Self-Help Assertiveness Program for Women and Men.* Willingborough: Thorsens, 1992.

Lloyd, S. *Developing Positive Assertiveness.* California: Crisp, 1988.

Luhn, R. R. *Managing Anger: Methods for a Happier and Healthier Life.* California: Crisp, 1992.

Luvmour, S. and J. Luvmour. *Everyone Wins: Cooperative Games and Activities.* British Columbia: New Society, 1990.

Maddux, Robert. *Team Building: An Exercise In Leadership.* California: Crisp, 1986.

McFarland, Rhonda: *Coping Through Assertiveness.* New York: Rosen, 1986.

Mangini, Shirley. *Secrets of Self Esteem.* New York: Bantam, 1991.

Mattox, Beverly. *Getting It Together: Dilemmas For The Classroom.* California: Pennant, 1975.

Minor, M. *Coaching and Counselling: A Practical Guide for Managers.* California: Crisp, 1989.

Morris, J. *Pride against Prejudice: Transforming Attitudes to Disability.* British Columbia: New Society, 1991.

Morris, Kenneth and Kenneth Cinnamon. *A Handbook Of Non Verbal Group Exercises.* Missouri: Applied Skills, 1975.

Morris, Kenneth and Kenneth Cinnamon. *A Handbook of Verbal Group Exercises.* Missouri: Applied Skills, 1979.

Nilson, Carolyn. *Team Games for Trainers.* New York: McGraw-Hill, 1993.

O'Connell, April, and Vincent O'Connell. *Choice And Change: The Psychology of Adjustment Growth and Creativity.* New Jersey: Prentice Hall, 1980.

O'Connell, April, and Vincent O'Connell. *Choice And Change: Study Guide.* New Jersey: Prentice Hall, 1980.

Palladino, C. *Developing Self-Esteem: A Positive Guide for Personal Success.* California: Crisp, 1989.

Parker, Glenn and Richard Kropp. *Fifty Activities For Team Building. Vol 1.* Massachusetts: HRD, 1989.

Parker, Glenn and Richard Kropp. *Fifty Activities For Team Building. Vol. 2.* Massachusetts: HRD, 1992.

Peavy, R.V. *Counselling Adults For Decision Making.* Toronto: Guidance Centre, University of Toronto, 1984.

Pfeiffer, J. William, ed. *Developing Human Resources (1972-1995 editions).* California: Pfeiffer.

Pfeiffer, J. William. ed. *The Encyclopedia of Group Activities.* California: University Associates, 1989.

Pfeiffer, J. William, ed. *The Encyclopedia Of Team Building Activities.* California: University Associates, 1991.

Pfeiffer, J. William. ed. *The Encyclopedia Of Team Development Activities.* California: University Associates, 1991.

Pfeiffer, J. William. ed. *A Handbook of Structured Experiences For Human Relations Training, Vol. I-X.* California: University Associates.

Pfeiffer and Company. *Addressing Sexual Harassment in the Workplace: Trainers Package.* California: 1992.

Phillips, Kenneth. *Problem-Solving Style Inventory.* Pennsylvania: Organization Design and Development, 1986.

Pickle Lake Development Project. *Life Skills For Employment.* Thunder Bay Ontario: Confederation College.

Pollar, O. and R. Gonzalez. *Dynamics of Diversity: Strategic Programs for Your Organization.* California: Crisp, 1994.

Pokras, S. *Systematic Problem-Solving and Decision-Making.* California: Crisp, 1989.

Raudsepp, Eugene. *Creative Growth Games.* New York: Perigree, 1977.

Raudsepp, Eugene. *More Creative Growth Games.* New York: Perigee, 1980.

Raudsepp, Eugene. *How Creative Are You?* New York: Perigree, 1981.

Renner, Peter. *The Instructor's Survival Kit: A Handbook for Teachers of Adults.* British Columbia: PER Training Associates, 1991.

Saint, S. and J.R. Lawson. *Rules for Reaching Consensus: A Modern Approach to Decision Making.* California: Pfeiffer, 1994.

Sandford, Linda Tschirhart and Mary Ellen Donovan. *Women and Self Esteem.* New York: Penguin, 1984.

Saskin, Marshal and W. C. Morris. *PIPS: Phase of Integrated Problem-Solving.* Organization Design and Development, 1985.

Saskin, Marshal *The Visionary Leader: Questionnaire.* Organization Design and Development, 1985.

Saskin, Marshal *The Visionary Leader: Trainer Guide.* Organization Design and Development, 1985.

Sasse, Connie. *Person To Person: Teacher's Guide.* Illinois: Bennett and McKnight, 1981.

Sax, Seville and Sandra Hollander. *Reality Games.* Toronto: Macmillan, 1975.

Scannell, Edward, and John Newstrom. *Games Trainers Play: Experiential Learning Exercises.* New York: McGraw-Hill, 1980.

Scannell, Edward and John Newstrom. *More Games Trainers Play: Experiential Learning Exercises.* New York: McGraw-Hill, 1983.

Scannell, Edward and John Newstrom. *Still More Games Trainers Play: Experiential Learning Exercises.* New York: McGraw-Hill, 1991.

Shackelton, V.J. et al. *Survival: The Impact Of Leadership Style.* California: University Associates, 1982.

Sher, Barbara, and Annie Gottlieb. *Wishcraft: How To Get What You Really Want.* New York: Ballantine, 1979.

Silberman, Mel. *Active Training: A Handbook of Techniques, Designs, Case Examples and Tips.* California: Pfeiffer, 1990.

Silberman, Mel. *101 Ways to Make Training Active.* California: Pfeiffer, 1995.

Silberman, Mel, ed. *Twenty Active Training Programs.* California: Pfeiffer and Co., 1992.

Simon, Sidney, et al. *Values Clarification: A Handbook of Practical Strategies for Teachers and Students.* New York: Hart, 1972.

Simons, G.F. *Working Together: How to Become More Effective in a Multicultural Organization.* California: Crisp, 1989.

Smith, D. and L.K. Williamson. *Interpersonal Communication: Roles, Rules, Strategies and Games.* Iowa: Brown, 1977.

Smith, J. *Creative Stress Management: The 1-2-3 Cope System.* New Jersey: Prentice Hall, 1993.

Suessmuth, P. *Training Ideas Found Useful.* Winnipeg, Manitoba: Paracan, 1986.

Thayer, Louis. *Fifty Strategies For Experiential Learning, (Book 1)*. California: University Associates, 1976.

Thayer, Louis. *Fifty Strategies For Experiential Learning, (Book 2)*. California: University Associates, 1981.

Tubesing, Donald. *Kicking Your Stress Habits*. Minnesota: Whole Person, 1982.

Tubesing, Donald. *The Whole Person Guide to Teaching About Stress*. Minnesota: Whole Person, 1989.

Tubesing, Nancy and Donald Tubesing. *The Caring Question*. Augsburg: Whole Person, 1983.

Tubesing, Nancy and Donald Tubesing. *Structured Exercises In Stress Management, (Volumes I-V)*. Minnesota: Whole Person, 1988.

Tubesing, Nancy and Donald Tubesing. *Structured Exercises In Wellness Promotion, (Volumes I-V)*. Minnesota: Whole Person, 1988.

Vineyard Ben and Katherine Vineyard. *Choosing the Right Career*. Illinois: Bennett and Knight, 1984.

Warren, Nell. *The Warmups Manual*. Toronto: Nell Warren Associates, 1990.

Warren, Nell. *The Warmups Manual II*. Toronto: Nell Warren Associates, 1992.

Watkinson, Susan. *Life Skills Coaching Manual: A Continuous Intake Dacum Approach*. Toronto: 1974.

Women's Self-Help Network, ed. *Women's Self Help Handbook. Vol. I and II*. British Columbia: North Island Women's Service Society, 1984.

Women's Self-Help Network, ed. *Working Together For Change*. British Columbia: North Island Women's Service Society, 1984.

Woodrow, P. *Clearness: Processes for Supporting Individuals and Groups in Decision Making*. Pennsylvania: New Society, 1986.

NOTES

NOTES

NOTES

NOTES

NOTES

NOTES